MEDITERRANEAN DIET COOKBOOK FOR BEGINNERS

2000+ DAYS OF QUICK AND EASY RECIPES TO GET STARTED WITH A MEDITERRANEAN EATING LIFESTYLE AND LOSE WEIGHT | 30 DAY MEAL PLAN (HD COLOR EDITION)

SOPHIA LEWIS

ABOUT THE AUTHOR

Sophia Lewis is a sports nutritionist, chef, and author, born in Italy in 1982 and raised in Brooklyn since age three.

Through her family's Italian roots and their love for good food made with love and quality ingredients, Lewis was able to form healthy eating habits from an early age. However, she found that the same is not true for her friends and peers.

With this realization, she sought training at her family's Italian restaurant and then a culinary education at The Culinary Institute of America to pursue a career as a personal chef, with a focus on specialized diets. Her goal is to bridge the gap between healthy eating and colorful Italian flavors.

Throughout her life, Lewis believes that a well-balanced diet will never lead to obesity — one of the US's leading epidemics.

By working with fellow chefs and researchers, Lewis has found compelling links between a healthier weight and the Mediterranean diet. Not one to be swayed by trends, Lewis applied the same principles in her family's meals and found that not only were her three children and husband healthier, they also regained lost vitality and boosted their metabolism.

Today, Lewis has made her learning more accessible to people who want to eat better and live healthier without having to spend hours in the kitchen through her bestselling books. And she's been delighted with the developments in her readers' lives ever since.

If you're willing to put in the work for a healthier, fitter, more energized you, then you're exactly who Lewis wants to help. Grab a copy of her books today, available in black-and-white and colored versions.

TABLE OF CONTENTS

CHAPTER 5: 36 MEDITERRANEAN LUNCH RECIPES 47

INTRODUCTION

If you have been seeking to identify palatable meals which not only make you full but also trim and healthy, this book is for you. You will find in here a wide range of recipes from the Mediterranean diet; a diet that is gaining popularity by the day. Though many people have only recently learnt of this healthy diet, it used to be the diet for many traditional cultures; the reason these people lived long healthy lives.

It is unfortunate that despite the goodness of the Mediterranean diet being backed by science, a lot of confusion still lingers regarding this mode of feeding. Granted the diet is becoming more and more popular, but the information available seems to be laden with inconsistencies and inaccuracies.

This book is meant to provide you with accurate and reliable information pertaining to the Mediterranean diet, which will help you to eat healthy meals on a daily basis, and to lead a long happy life. This information comprises breakfast recipes, lunch and dinner recipes, as well as salads.

Moreover, these recipes have detailed procedures on how to prepare the meals, which are easy to understand and implement. You will particularly like the richness of the information provided all through the book, which is a result of well done research, and studies pertaining to people's authentic feeding patterns.

CHAPTER 1:

MEANING OF MEDITERRANEAN DIET

The Mediterranean diet is a diet with extraordinary health benefits. It is representative of a way of life whose fundamentals include consumption of plenty of unprocessed fruits, fresh vegetables, fish and other seafood, as well as generous use of extra virgin olive oil.

The Mediterranean diet is a great way of leading a healthy life free from meat, or at least consuming meat in minimal amounts.

People began to appreciate in depth the benefits of consuming the Mediterranean diet over half a decade ago, and people began to increase their daily consumption of fruits and vegetables and also extra virgin olive oil.

This diet is credited with longevity of life, with people relying on the diet getting to attain the age of ninety. One of the notable benefits of the Mediterranean diet is that the risk of heart disease and incidences of obesity are greatly reduced.

Reliance on the Mediterranean diet was adopted from the impressive lifestyle of the people of Crete, one of several Greek islands. Although the Cretans were the originators of this diet, many of the inhabitants of the Mediterranean region were quick to appreciate and adopt it.

As such, the Mediterranean diet is consumed widely not only in Greece, but also in the southern parts of Italy and France, as well as in some areas of the Middle East and Northern Africa.

One of the reasons people reliant on the Mediterranean diet rarely encounter ailments of the heart and other cholesterol related diseases is that many of the ingredients used are light. This is in great contrast to situations where people are reliant on foods rich in saturated fats. People who are heavy consumers of meat and animal products like fat-rich cheese often suffer heart diseases; as is the case in countries like the USA and other Western countries.

Besides being rich in helpful nutrients, Mediterranean foods have great fragrance and are easy to prepare. Many of these foods are great when grilled, especially when accompanied with varied spices such as basil, sage, thyme, rosemary, oregano, ginger, caraway, and others like those in the mint family.

Well made Mediterranean foods do not only help you reach satiety levels fast, but they also keep you continually healthy.

Brief History of the Mediterranean Diet

People derived the concept of the Mediterranean diet from the traditional feeding habits of the people who live around the Mediterranean Sea. These people include those in Spain and France, Italy and Greece, Morocco, Lebanon and Tunisia. Considering the peoples of these countries do not necessary have similar cultures, it is not surprising that today's Mediterranean diet comprises a range of palatable foods.

In short, you are able to stick to the Mediterranean diet while still enjoying varieties of dishes. This also means that you have room to enjoy the benefits of a wide range of food ingredients while still sticking to this age-old diet.

It is probably for this reason that the eating habits of people around the regions of the Mediterranean Sea have not changed in any significant way for hundreds of years.

Hence, people of these areas have continued to enjoy longer and healthier lives compared to those from parts of the world who depend on more modern diets.

The Mediterranean diet as it is presented today was brought to the fore by one American physician during the 1940s, but real prominence of the diet was noted during the 1990s. Popularization of the diet began as a simple recommendation by doctors to anyone intent on losing weight.

Why Mediterranean Diet is Considered Healthy

The Mediterranean diet is considered healthy because it constitutes a balanced diet while lacking the harmful ingredients of modern foods. In comparison, the Mediterranean diet is free from refined sugars and foods that produce bad cholesterol.

Instead, the diet mainly comprises fresh fruits, fresh vegetables, olive oil, fish and nuts. This range of ingredients has capacity to drastically reduce the risk of heart ailments such as high blood pressure and stroke; debilitating illness like Alzheimer's and Parkinson's disease; and also type II diabetes and live ailments. The ingredients even reduce the risk of developing cancer.

Besides, people remain agile as long as they are living on the Mediterranean diet.

Heart Health

Keeping your heart and the blood vessels healthy is very important, because failure to do so may raise your risk of developing heart disease or even type II diabetes.

As long as your blood vessels are working normally, blood will continue to flow optimally within the different systems of your body. For example, when a large volume of blood is needed, the vessels will enlarge appropriately.

In the event there is need to have a large volume of blood pumped but the blood vessels happen to be rigid, the heart will have to exert more pressure for the sake of pumping blood through those vessels. Such increased force or pressure can lead to heart failure.

If there is excessive pressure within the arteries, this too can cause out-pouching that resembles balloons, which can eventually lead to stroke. Other times such out-pouching can lead to other forms of internal bleeding after rupturing of some blood vessel.

The risk of developing such problems of the heart is mitigated once you make the Mediterranean diet part of your lifestyle. This means consuming vegetables and fruits on a daily basis, and ensuring your meals have such ingredients whole grains, seeds and nuts, as well as beans.

Weight Regulation

The Mediterranean diet helps you maintain a healthy weight, hence minimizing the risk of obesity. Consequently, the diseases whose risk increases with weight are kept at bay.

Unfortunately, many people fall into the trap of putting themselves through some crash or fast-working diets, which cannot help sustain your required body weight. This means there is a large population of people who speak of dieting, yet their hope of a healthy life is soon shattered.

Of course during the first weeks of starting the diet they may experience weight loss, but they soon realize they cannot sustain it. Much of the initial loss does not happen only because of losing calories, but also due to dehydration.

Conversely, there are people who are not certain the Mediterranean diet has capacity to turn their lives around, only to have a pleasant surprise when they realize there is no strain when it comes to this traditional diet.

For one, the Mediterranean diet does not deprive anyone of any of nature's nutrients. For that reason, you rarely develop unhealthy cravings. You also do not find yourself overeating, because with this kind of diet your satiety level is healthy for your body.

So, in comparison, crash diets are likely to put you in a vicious cycle, where you lose weight and soon after regain it – sometimes more than you lost – while the Mediterranean diet is a sustainable way of life. Luckily, doctors all over the world are now in concurrence that the Mediterranean diet is healthy and worth recommending.

Cognitive Loss

Unhealthy feeding is one of the factors that could contribute to decline in the cognitive function. Luckily, the Mediterranean diet ensures the brain is well fed, just like all other parts of the body, and so all the body systems, including the neural system, have capacity to function optimally.

Among the health conditions involving cognitive decline is dementia, a condition that usually develops in individuals who are advanced in age. Dementia can be a result of Alzheimer's disease or other health conditions.

This health condition develops when protein deposits of an abnormal nature accumulate in the brain. They end up causing loss of connectivity among the neurons in the brain. Once that normal connectivity is lost, the neurons begin to die.

Making the Mediterranean diet your routine diet reduces in a significant way the risk of being cognitively impaired. This means you will find yourself scoring highly in the assessment of your cognitive function.

Fish is particularly recommended when it comes to minimizing risks of cognition loss. It is the food most credited with reducing the rate of cognitive decline.

Effect of Mediterranean Diet on Pregnancies

The Mediterranean diet has a rather indirect effect on pregnancies. While there is no direct correlation between maternal complications or those of the offspring, the diet contributes greatly to the overall health of both the mother and the unborn baby.

When a pregnant woman maintains healthy weight and takes in the required amount of nutrients, any risk of developing gestational diabetes and such other illnesses is mitigated.

In fact this diet is even more significant for women that become pregnant while already obese, or with the problem of hypertension.

It should be noted that any woman who becomes pregnant has potential to develop gestational diabetes. However, those that diabetes run in the family have a higher risk. Other women with potential to develop gestational diabetes are those over than 25yrs of age or have a BMI of 30. BMI stands for 'Body Mass Index'.

Benefits of Common Mediterranean Diet Spices

Considering the Mediterranean diet originated around the Mediterranean Sea, it is not surprising that many of the natural spices that form part of that diet thrive around that region. That may explain why people within the region tend to live long. In one of the Greek islands called Ikaria, for example, 90 years is the average life expectancy, with some residents living well over a hundred years.

It also needs to be mentioned that besides the great diet the people of these islands rely on, they also lead a healthy life pattern, where they walk around hence enhancing their physical wellbeing, and take a nap in the middle of the day to help the brain relax and rejuvenate. This healthy lifestyle is further boosted by the people's positive attitude to life. It also helps that many islanders lead relaxed lives as opposed to the fast and hectic lives of the Western world.

Composition of the Mediterranean Diet

The Mediterranean diet comprises protein foods, vegetables and fruits, prepared with or alongside natural spices. In fact, beans, grains, seeds, nuts and olive oil are a common feature in menus based on this diet.

Other foods that broaden the variety of the Mediterranean diet while maintaining its health benefits include eggs, poultry, fish and dairy products. Red meat, while acceptable, is expected to be consumed at a minimal level.

A list of common spices that have been used in Mediterranean recipes for centuries is provided here below. These spices have always enhanced the nutritional value and health benefits of the diet, but it is more so today that scientists have discovered how to take advantage of the antioxidant properties in the plants' polyphenols.

It has been discovered that steaming, simmering, boiling or stewing the spices enhances their antioxidant properties, hence making them better placed to improve people's health.

On the contrary, stir-frying or grilling spices reduces the antioxidant properties that otherwise make them valuable as part of the Mediterranean diet.

Basil

Basil is one of those spices with anti-microbial properties, especially as a natural antibiotic. It also has anti-inflammatory properties even as it helps to reduce unhealthy levels of cholesterol. Consequently, it is great for regulation of blood pressure.

Basil is also very helpful when one has a problem of water retention, and especially anyone with diabetes.

It also has antiseptic properties, and it helps to heal inflammation and certain forms of irritation. It is particularly great for people whose illnesses are around the gastric and renal areas, as well as within the intestines. Basil also enhances healing of coughs.

Another great health benefit of basil is its calming effect, which means the spice can help mitigate the stress that comes from a long day at work.

Basil, like many of the spices and herbs of the Mediterranean diet, is rich in polyphenols, which comprise a valuable category of antioxidants. In fact, 100g of dried basil contains 4,318mg of polyphenols.

Basil is popularly used in Mediterranean diet salads, as well as in pasta and tomato sauces. One of the very well known basil rich dishes is the Italian pesto.

The French also include basil in their popular herb collection referred to as 'Herbes de Provence'.

Thyme

As a herb, thyme comes in different sub-species; and all of them are great at enhancing the flavor and richness of Mediterranean dishes. The French commonly use it in their 'herbes de Provence' and also 'bouquet garni', both of which are herb collections.

The benefits of thyme are often derived from consuming its tea. This herb that serves as a tonic has great curative properties, and is particularly helpful to people with the problem of water retention.

100g of thyme contain 1,815mg of polyphenols.

Oregano

To Greeks, Oregano signifies joy. It is a spice with healthy oils that are volatile, and which help to deter proliferation of bacteria in the body.

Oregano also comes in a variety of sub-species, all of which are often used in dried form. This herb is usually among those used in the French 'bouquet garni'.

It medicinal value includes having anti-diabetes and anti-inflammatory properties. It is also hypolipidemic; meaning it tends to fight accumulation of bad cholesterol within the blood vessels.

Oregano also has antioxidant properties, with a single gram of the spice being forty-two times richer in anti-oxidation power than the coveted apple fruit.

The nutrients in Oregano include minerals such as iron and calcium, as well as vitamins A, C and K. It is also rich in omega 3 acids and fiber.

When it comes to polyphenols, there are 6,367mg of them in a single gram of Oregano. It is not surprising then that the spice has capacity to treat diarrhea and flatulence, and to destroy parasites that reside within the intestines.

Polyphenol level in Other Herbs & Spices

There are other herbs and spices that are rich in polyphenols, which means they are great at helping the body fight disease. These include bay leaf, which when dried has a polyphenol level of 4,170mg in a gram of spice.

Fennel is another of the polyphenol rich herbs and spices, which contains 3,949mg of polyphenols in a gram of dried spice.

As for sage, a gram of it in its dried state has 2,920mg of polyphenols, while a gram of dried rosemary contains 2,519mg of polyphenols.

As for dried cumin seeds, a gram of it contains 2,038mg of polyphenols, while a single gram of dried parsley contains 1,584mg of polyphenols.

Dried is also rich in polyphenols, and in its dried state a gram of it has 1,250mg of polyphenols.

Coriander seed also has a helpful level of polyphenols, with a gram of dried coriander having 357mg of polyphenols.

Bay Leaf

The bay leaf, which is commonly found in the southern parts of Europe, is usually included in dishes that are not only savory, but also sweet. This herb is also often included in the French 'bouquet garni'.

Other times, the bay leaf is made into a bundle, held together by use of a string, and then thrown into a pot to enhance the flavor and health value of the broth or stew.

Among the health benefits of bay leaf is having capacity to prevent and treat diabetes, lower unhealthy levels of cholesterol, and fight inflammation.

Coriander

Another name used to mean coriander leaves is cilantro. The seeds of the coriander plant are popular for their culinary value. They are especially liked in pickling. They are also often used to give a special flavor to sausages.

The health benefits of coriander include reduction of glucose levels in the blood and lowering levels of unhealthy cholesterol. This herb that is often preferred as a seed extract also helps in elimination of urine as well as enhancement of the kidney function.

Cumin

Cumin, which is also very common in the Mediterranean areas, is internationally accepted in culinary dishes.

Its seeds are usually ground and used in different dishes, especially those that have meat a major ingredient. The spice is also commonly used in pickles and sauces, and even in bread.

The major medicinal value of cumin seeds is their capacity to fight diabetes and to lower unhealthy levels of cholesterol.

Dill is a herb that belongs to the same family as celery. Its spice, which is very popular in pickling, is derived either from the plant or its seeds.

Besides enhancing meal flavor, dill also introduces healing properties. It is not only anti-diabetic but also hypolipidemic.

Fennel

The fennel is a very valuable herb, not only because it is a great component of the Mediterranean diet, but also because almost all its parts can be safely consumed – its leaves, seeds, leaves and even its bulb.

This herb introduces a nice flavor to salads, sausages and even bread, and it makes refreshing herbal tea.

It also has healing properties, which include fighting diabetes. It also reduces triglycerides and lowers unhealthy levels of cholesterol, even as it is said to have anti-inflammatory properties.

Parsley

Parsley, which is found in varying species, such as the curly leaf parsley, flat leaf parsley, Italian parsley and such other terms, is often used to garnish dishes. Other common culinary uses of parsley include being one of the ingredients in sauces, as well as in savory foods.

One Italian dish known for including parsley is the 'gremolata', and among French cuisines it is the 'persillade'. Both of these dishes have parsley that has been buttered and sautéed.

Parsley, which has capacity to fight diabetes, hypertension and inflammation, is also used as one of the herbs in 'bouquet garni' and also 'fines herbes'. It is rich in vitamin K, and therefore it is great at enhancing bone density; meaning it can help to keep osteoporosis at bay if consumed on a regular basis.

Rosemary

Rosemary is widely used when preparing French cuisines, and also when making 'bouquet garni'. It is also used in meat dishes and soups.

As for its medicinal value, this herb has properties that fight bacteria, viruses as well as fungus. Also if it is consumed on a regular basis, it fights inflammation.

Sage

Sage is popularly used to flavor sausages and soups, and also as one of the ingredients in bouquet garni".

The healing properties of sage include fighting diabetes and hypertension, as well as inflammation. The herb is also used to treat problems of digestion, inhibited appetite and heartburn.

Tarragon

Tarragon is typically French, and is commonly used in sauces like the béarnaise and the béchamel. It is also used to flavor chicken.

Tarragon is also one of the herbs that make the list of those making servings of 'bouquet garni'.

Sometimes this herb is steeped in vinegar and even oil such as olive, for purposes of preparing salad dressing.

In terms of medicinal value, tarragon is primarily credited with helping to prevent and treat diabetes.

CHAPTER 2:
MEAL PLAN

	BREAKFAST	LUNCH	DINNER	SNACK
Monday	Bowl of Strawberry, Thyme & Millet	Lettuce Chickpeas Wraps	Roasted Portobello Mushroom Pizza	Rosemary-Garlic Pecans
Tuesday	Blueberry Almond Milk Smoothie	Chicken, Cucumber & Quinoa Recipe	Olives, Ravioli & Artichokes	Homemade Trail Mix
Wednesday	Feta & Watermelon Radish Toast	Prosciutto & Herbs	Slow-cooking Quinoa & Arugula	Fig & Honey Yogurt
Thursday	Tomato Toast, Mint Yorghurt & Sumack Vinaigrette	Pita-Salmon-Watercress Sanwich	Crusted Salmon with Walnut & Rosemary	Savory Date & Pistachio Bites
Friday	Cauliflower-rich 'Tabbouleh'	Greek Vegetable-rich Meatball	Spaghetti Squash stuffed with Cheesy Spinach plus Artichoke	Lime & Parmesan Popcorn
Saturday	Avocado-Banana Smoothie	Lentil & Cucumber Salad	Chicken Breasts stuffed with Feta Cheese	Apricot-Sunflower Granola Bars
Sunday	Tacos of Scrambled Eggs	Quinoa, Nuts & Feta salad with Cherry tomatoes	Pesto, Shrimp & Quinoa	Carrot Cake Energy Bites

	BREAKFAST	LUNCH	DINNER	SNACK
Monday	Peach, Mango & Carrot Smoothie	Chickpeas & Red Pepper Soup	Salmon, Broccoli & Sweet potatoes	Date Pistachio Granola Bars
Tuesday	Egg Muffins of Goat Cheese plus Spinach	Broccoli, Kale, Beans & Yogurt	Slow-cooked Mediterranean Stew	Garlic Hummus
Wednesday	Delicious Shakshuka	Fruit & Vegetable Salad with Feta Cheese & Walnuts	Grilled Chicken, Greek Cauliflower & Rice	Everything Seasoned Almonds
Thursday	Mango-Banana Smoothie	Kale, Couscous & Basil Vinaigrette	Arugula, Prosciutto Pizza & Corn	Seneca White Corn No Bake Energy Balls
Friday	Spinach with Curry Crepes	Hummus & Greek Salad with Feta Cheese	Vegan Lentil Soup	Kale Chips
Saturday	Herb-based Frittata	Prosciutto, Baguette & Mozzarella balls with Strawberry	Eggplant-based Parmesan	Curried Cashew
Sunday	Bruschetta with Nectarine	Mediterranean-type Wraps	BBQ Shrimp, Kale with Garlic & Parmesan Couscous	Tuna Salad Spread

	BREAKFAST	LUNCH	DINNER	SNACK
Monday	Banana-Blueberry Smoothie	Grilled Turkey, Pita Bread & Grapes	Salmon, Fennel & Tomato Couscous	Rosemary-Garlic Pecans
Tuesday	Omelette with Cheese & Avocado	Chicken & Cucumber stuffed Pita with Greek Yogurt	Chicken, Spinach, Parmesan & Skillet Pasta	Homemade Trail Mix
Wednesday	Vegetable Mix & Sweet Potatoes	Slow Cooking Chicken thighs & Peas with Fresh Herbs	Chicken pea, Quinoa, Chick pea salad & Vegetables	Fig & Honey Yogurt
Thursday	Banana-Whole Wheat Pancakes	Mediterranean Pasta with Hummus & Baby Kale	Chicken, Gnocchi & Brussels Sprouts	Savory Date & Pistachio Bites
Friday	Coconut milk Yogurt	Peppery Quinoa with Chickpea & Almonds	Portobello Mushrooms with Caprese	Lime & Parmesan Popcorn
Saturday	Cauliflower & Strawberry Smoothie	Mediterranean Sweet Peppers, Kale and Lentils	Roasted Salmon (sweet & spicy) & Wild Rice Pilaf	Apricot-Sunflower Granola Bars
Sunday	Milky Pumpkin Bread	Tabbouleh, Hummus, Berries with Pita Bread	Smoked Mozzarella & Rolls of Zucchini Lasagna	Carrot Cake Energy Bites

	BREAKFAST	LUNCH	DINNER	SNACK
Monday	Vegan Milky Banana Muffins	Garlic-rich Cheese Ravioli & Vegetable Broth	Mediterranean Fish, Mushrooms & Wilted Greens	Date Pistachio Granola Bars
Tuesday	Garlicky Quiche	Chicken Salad & Greek Yogurt with Pesto	Chicken & Tomato-Balsamic Sauce	Garlic Hummus
Wednesday	Instant Oatmeal	Tuna salad with Spinach & Orange	Baked Ravioli, Mushroom Bolognese plus Red Pepper	Everything Seasoned Almonds
Thursday	Cauliflower-based Smoothie	Chicken Salad with Edamame & Feta Cheese	Seared Halibut, Tomatoes & Corn with Cream	Seneca White Corn No Bake Energy Balls
Friday	Chia & Pumpkin Seeds Granola	Mixed Greens, Tomatoes, Beans & Cucumber	Greek Burgers & Herb-rich Feta Sauce	Kale Chips
Saturday	Cheesy Chia seed Meatballs	Broccoli, Bell Peppers & Pesto with Brown Rice	Roast Fish & Vegetables	Curried Cashew
Sunday	Fruity Chia seed Pops	Shrimp, Beet & Arugula-rich Salad	Easy Pea with Spinach Carbonara	Tuna Salad Spread

CHAPTER 3: INDEX

DINNER RECIPES

SALADS

MEDITERRANEAN DIET

CHAPTER 4:

31 MEDITERRANEAN BREAKFAST RECIPES

BOWL OF STRAWBERRY, THYME & MILLET

INGREDIENTS: (4 SERVINGS)

Strawberries (hulled & diced into halves) – 1 pound

Thyme (fresh) – 4 sprigs

Olive oil – 1 tbsp

Honey – 1 tbsp

Milk – 1 cup (& a little extra)

Millet – 1 cup

Vanilla extract (pure) – 1½ tsp

Pistachios (well chopped) – 2 tbsp

Hemp seeds – 2 tbsp

Water – 1 cup

METHOD OF PREPARATION: (TOTAL TIME TAKEN: 45 MINUTES)

1st Step

Pre-heat oven up to 450° F. Take a baking sheet and pour the strawberries on it. Add the thyme, honey & the oil. ssPut in the oven and bake for around 10 minutes (the berries should release their juices). Take the baking sheet out of the oven & get rid of the thyme.

2nd Step

Put the milk into a sauce pan and add a cup of water. Heat until the milky liquid boils. Add in the millet & the vanilla and stir. Lower the heat and let the contents simmer while covered. Cook for between 25 & 30 minutes (the liquid should be absorbed and the millet tender)

3rd Step

Serve the millet dish alongside the berries & the juices in the pan, and add a tiny amount of milk. . Serve also the pistachios and the hemp seeds.

Nutrition per Single Serving

358 cal/11g protein/54g carbohydrates/7g fiber/14.5g sugar (4.5g added)/11g fat (2g saturated)/6mg cholesterol/37mg sodium.

BLUEBERRY ALMOND MILK SMOOTHIE

INGREDIENTS: (2 SERVINGS)

Blueberries (frozen) – 1 cup

Almond (unsweetened) milk – ½ cup

Protein Powder – 1½ scoops

Almond butter (unsweetened) – 2 tsp

Vanilla extract (pure) – 1 tsp

Blueberries (fresh) – ½ cup

Vanilla granola – ¼ cup

Almonds (sliced – 2 tbsp

Hemp seeds – 2 tsp

Cinnamon (ground) – 1 tsp

METHOD OF PREPARATION: (TOTAL TIME TAKEN: 10 MINUTES)

Use a blender to puree the blueberries and the almond milk, alongside the protein powder, vanilla & almond butter, until a creamy mixture is formed. . Share the creamy liquid between 2 bowls. Take the blueberries, cinnamon and the granola, together with the almonds and hemp seeds, and spread them on top of the contents in each of the 2 bowls . Now serve.

Nutrition per Single Serving

370cal/25g protein/32g carbs/7g fiber/16g sugar(4g added)/17g fat(2.5g saturated)/0mg cholesterol/130mg sodium

FETA & WATERMELON RADISH TOAST

INGREDIENTS: (4 SERVINGS)

Feta cheese (cut into bits) – 3oz

Milk – 2 tbsp

Sour dough toast – 4 slices (thick)

Watermelon radish (finely sliced) – 1

Red radish (finely sliced) – 2

Broccoli sprouts – ½ cup

Olive oil – your preference

Kosher salt – your preference

Pepper – your preference

METHOD OF PREPARATION: (TOTAL TIME TAKEN: 10 MINUTES)

In a small food processor, put in the feta cheese plus the milk and puree to make smooth. Keep adding milk during the process, as is necessary. Spread that puree on the toast slices. Add the watermelon radish on top. Next add the red radish. Add the broccoli sprouts on top. Take the olive oil and sprinkle it on top. Finally sprinkle some salt & pepper and serve.

Nutrition per Single Serving

278 cal/11g protein/37g carbs/2g fiber/3.5g sugar(none added)/9.5g fat(4g saturated)/20mg cholesterol/676mg sodium.

TOMATO TOAST, MINT YORGHURT & SUMACK VINAIGRETTE

INGREDIENTS: (4 SERVINGS)

Greek yorghurt – ½ cup

Scallion (well chopped) – 1 (plus some extra to serve with)

Mint (roughly chopped) – ¼ cup

Lemon zest (grated) – 2 tsp

Olive oil – 2 tbsp

Lemon juice – 1 tsp

Cumin seed – ¼ tsp

Sumac (ground) – ¼ tsp

Pepper (roughly cracked) – ¼ tsp

Kosher salt – ¼ tsp

Bread (toasted) – 4 pcs

Heirloom tomatoes (medium & sliced) – 3

METHOD OF PREPARATION: (TOTAL TIME TAKEN: 10 MINUTES)

Pour into a bowl the Greek yogurt & lemon zest. Add in the scallion & the mint and mix. Take a 2nd bowl and in it put the olive oil and the lemon juice. Add in the cumin seed, sumac, pepper & the salt and whisk the contents. Take the yogurt and spread it on the toasts. Add on top the heirloom tomatoes. On the tomatoes, lay the spoon vinaigrette. Take some more scallion and sprinkle on top as you wish before serving.

Nutrition per Single Serving

182 cal/8g protein/17g carbs/4g fiber/5.5g sugar (none added)/10g fat(2g saturated)/4mg cholesterol/243mg sodium.

CAULIFLOWER-RICH 'TABBOULEH'

INGREDIENTS: (4 SERVINGS)

Cauliflower (raw florets) – 12oz

Parsley (curly with stems; then chopped) – 1 cup

Cherry tomatoes (in halves) – 1 cup

Persian cucumbers (in slices) – 2

Lemon juice (fresh) – 3 tbsp

Red onion (small & well chopped) – ½

Cumin (ground) – ½ tsp

Kosher salt – ½ tsp

Pepper – ½ tsp

METHOD OF PREPARATION: (TOTAL TIME TAKEN: 20 MINUTES)

1st Step

Making of Cauliflower rice.Put the cauliflower in the food processor and chop it finely to make 2½ cups. Pour the contents into a big bowl.

2nd Step

Use the processor to finely chop the parsley. Transfer the chopped parsley to the bowl that has the cauliflower. Add in the tomatoes, the cucumbers and the red onion. Add in the cumin, pepper, salt & lemon juice and toss to mix all ingredients. Modify the seasoning if you deem fit and proceed to serve.

Nutrition per Single Serving

47 calories/10g carbs/3g fiber/3.5g sugar (none added)/0.5g fat (non saturated)/no cholesterol/ 278mg sodium.

NB

Cauliflower here is used in place of whole grains.

AVOCADO-BANANA SMOOTHIE

INGREDIENTS: (2 SERVINGS)

Avocado – ½

Ripe banana – 1

Spinach – 1 cup

Milk – 1 cup (250ml)

Dates (optional & pitted) – 2

METHOD OF PREPARATION: (TOTAL TIME TAKEN: 5 MINUTES)

Put the ingredients into a blender. Process until the mixture is smooth. Serve with toppings of your preference.

Nutrition per Single Serving

178 cal/8g sugar/2.5g protein/19.3g carbs/11.6g fat (2.1g saturated)/5.7g fiber105mg sodium

TACOS OF SCRAMBLED EGGS

INGREDIENTS: (4 SERVINGS)

Olive oil – 2 tbsp

Black beans (rinsed) – 1 can (15oz)

Cumin seeds – ½ tsp

Garlic (nicely chopped) – 1 clove

Kosher salt – your preference

Pepper – your preference

Baby spinach – 4 cups

Lemon juice (fresh) – 1 tbsp

Eggs – 8 (big ones)

Tortillas (from yellow corn) – 8

Sour cream - your preference

Queso fresco (crumbled) – your preference

Cilantro (your preference)

METHOD OF PREPARATION: (TOTAL TIME TAKEN: 15 MINUTES)

Take a big skillet in pour in 1 tablespoon oil . Add in the beans, garlic & the cumin. Use 1/8 tsp salt plus 1/8 tsp pepper for seasoning. Cook the contents for around 2 minutes. (The garlic should begin to appear golden brown). Add in the spinach and take the skillet off the heat. Toss contents until the leaves are close to wilting. Pour in the lemon juice and stir. Break the eggs into a bowl and whisk them. Add in 1 tbsp of water plus ½ tsp of salt & pepper & whisk the mixture. Take a non-stick skillet of medium size and pour in the remainder of the oil . Add in the egg mixture & cook for between 2 & 3 minutes; in the meantime use some rubber spatula to keep stirring (how done the egg becomes is your choice). Char the tortillas lightly using either a broiler or some gas flame. Take the beans and eggs as well as the sour cream, cilantro & the queso fresco and use them to fill the tortillas.

Nutrition per Single Serving

478 calories/29g protein/46g carbs/9g fiber/0.5g sugar(none added)/18.5g fat(4g saturated)/372mg cholesterol/961mg sodium.

PEACH, MANGO & CARROT SMOOTHIE

INGREDIENTS: (2 SERVINGS)

Peach (ripe, peeled & chopped) – 1

Mango (ripe, peeled & chopped) – 1

Carrots (peeled & chopped) – 2

Lime juice – 2½ tsp

Almond milk (unsweetened) – ½ cup

Flaxseed (optional)

METHOD OF PREPARATION: (TOTAL TIME TAKEN: 8 MINUTES)

Put all the ingredients into a blender. Process until the mixture becomes smooth; then serve.

Nutrition per Single Serving

185 cal/45g carbs/4g protein/3g fat (0.3g saturated)/40g sugars/8g fiber/100mg sodium/95mg calcium/1mg iron/710mg potassium

EGG MUFFINS OF GOAT CHEESE PLUS SPINACH

INGREDIENTS: (12 SERVINGS)

Olive oil – 1 tbsp

Red pepper (split into big pieces) – 1 (big)

Kosher salt & pepper – as needed

Scallions (well chopped) – 2

Eggs (big) – 6

Milk – ½ cup

Baby spinach (chopped) – l package (5oz)

Goat cheese (fresh & crumbled) – ¼ cup

METHOD OF PREPARATION: (TOTAL TIME TAKEN: 45 MINUTES)

1st Step

Pre-heat the oven up to 350° F

Take a muffin pan (to fit 12 cups) and apply cooking spray

2nd Step

Take a big skillet and pour in the oil. Place the skillet over medium heat. Add in the red pepper, 1/8 tsp salt & 1/8 tsp pepper. Cover the skillet and cook the contents for between 6 & 8 min, and stir occasionally (peppers should become tender). Take the skillet off the heat, add in the scallions and stir.

3rd Step

Break the eggs into a big bowl & beat them. Add in the milk, ¼ tsp salt, 1/8 tsp pepper, and whisk. Add in the spinach . Next add in the mixture with red pepper and stir properly.

4th Step

Divide that egg mixture among the 12 muffin cups and top them with the cheese.. Bake the contents for between 20 & 25 min (the mixture should be set at the middle). Proceed to cook the muffins for 5 min on the wire rack, and then take out the pan. Serve when still warm.

NB:

Even after the frittatas are set around the center, they may appear wet because of the spinach in them

The ready muffins may be refrigerated for a period of even 4 days, and before they are served they can be put on high-level heat in the microwave for 30 sec.

Nutrition per Single Serving

65 cal/4g protein/2g carbs/1g fiber/1g sugar (none added)/4.5g fat (1.5g saturated)/97mg cholesterol/120mg sodium.

DELICIOUS SHAKSHUKA

INGREDIENTS: (4 SERVINGS)

Olive oil – 2 tbsp

Onion (well chopped) – 1

Garlic (well chopped) – 1 clove

Cumin (ground) – 1 tsp

Kosher salt – as needed

Pepper – as needed

Tomatoes (cherry & Campari; can be cut if big) – 1 pound

Eggs (big) – 8

Basil (fresh & well chopped) – ¼ cup

Baguette (toasted) – to be served alongside main dish.

METHOD OF PREPARATION: (TOTAL TIME TAKEN: 35 MINUTES)

1st Step

Pre-heat oven up to 400° F.

2nd Step

Pour the oil in a big skillet and heat it over medium heat. Sauté the onion for 8 minutes (it should become tender & golden brown). Add in the garlic, the cumin, ½tsp salt & ½tsp pepper & then stir. Cook contents for 1 minute. Add in the tomatoes and stir. Transfer the contents to the oven & let it roast for 10 minutes.

3rd Step

Stir the vegetables. Create 8 tiny wells within the vegetable mix; then break into every one of them one egg. Put the contents back into the oven for between 7 & 8 minutes, so that the eggs can bake as needed (yolks should remain a bit runny). Take the basil & sprinkle it on the dish. Serve the dish with some toast.

Nutrition per Single Serving

237 calories/14g protein/8g carbs/2g fiber/4.5g sugar (none added)/16.5g fat (4g saturated)/372 mg cholesterol/392mg sodium.

MANGO-BANANA SMOOTHIE

INGREDIENTS: (1 SERVINGS)

Mango (frozen chunks) – 1 cup (140g)

Ripe banana (big, chopped & frozen) – 1

Milk (without sweetening) – ½ cup (125ml)

METHOD OF PREPARATION: (TOTAL TIME TAKEN: 5 MINUTES)

Put the ingredients into a strong blender. Process until the mixture becomes smooth. Serve.

Nutrition per Single Serving

276 cal/3.5g protein/67.1g carbs/47.1g sugars/1.7g fat (0.2g saturated)/7.6g fiber/54mg sodium

SPINACH WITH CURRY CREPES

INGREDIENTS: (6 SERVINGS)

Eggs – 2

Cilantro (fresh & chopped) – 1/3 cup

Black pepper – ¼ tsp

Milk – 2½ cups

Flour (all purpose) – 1 cup

Safflower oil – 3 tbsp

Kosher salt – ¾ tsp

Yellow onion (small & chopped) – 1

Chickpeas (rinsed then drained) – 1 can (15.5oz)

Green apple (well diced) – 1

Golden raisins – ¼ cup

Curry powder (Madras) – 2 tbsp

Spinach (fresh) – 10 oz

Lemon – in wedges to serve along

METHOD OF PREPARATION: (TOTAL TIME TAKEN: 40 MINUTES)

1st Step

Into a blender put in the eggs & the cilantro, as well as the pepper, flour, a cup of milk, 2 tablespoons of oil plus ¼ teaspoon of salt.. Blend the mixture into puree

2nd Step

Take a non-stick skillet and apply some cooking spray. Heat the skillet on medium. Next pour in 1/3 of the prepared batter, ensuring it is evenly spread. Cook the mixture for a minute (the edges should be set). Flip the batter and let it cook for a further 30 sec.

3rd Step

Repeat the process for the balance of the crepes; then cover to keep them warm.

4th Step

Heat the balance of the oil (1 tbsp) in a skillet on medium. Add in the onion; then cook for 5 min (onion should be soft). Add in the chickpeas and the apple, the raisins plus the curry powder. Cook contents for 3 min. Add in the balance of the flour (2 tbsp), stir and cook for a further 30 sec.. Add in the balance of the milk (1½ cups) and then stir the contents. Cook for a further 2 min (mixture should be thick). Add in the spinach plus the balance of the salt (½ tsp). Cook for 2 min (spinach should be wilted). Share the contents among the crepes; then fold them into halves. Serve the breakfast alongside the lemon wedges.

Nutrition per Single Serving

327 calories/13g protein/47g carbs/6g fiber/13g sugar/11g fat (2g saturated)/541mg sodium

HERB-BASED FRITTATA

INGREDIENTS: (4 SERVINGS)

Crème fraiche (room temperature) – ¼ cup

Chives (well chopped) – 2 tbsp

Eggs – 6

Scallions (diced into pieces, 1" thick) – 6

Parsley (leaves only) – 2 cups (& a little extra)

Cilantro (leaves plus stem if tender) – 2 cups (& a little extra)

Dill fronds – ½ cup (& a little extra)

Olive oil – 4 tbsp

Kosher salt – as needed

Pepper – as needed

METHOD OF PREPARATION: (TOTAL TIME TAKEN: 40 MINUTES)

1st Step

Pre-heat oven up to 350° F. Put the crème fraiche together with the chives and stir them. Then refrigerate them until the time of use.

2nd Step

Break the eggs into a bowl and beat them lightly

3rd Step

Put the pulse scallions in a food processor . Add in the cilantro and the dill; as well as 2 tbsp of oil. Process to ensure everything is finely cut and evenly distributed

4th Step

Pour the processed mixture into the bowl that contains eggs. Add in ½ tsp salt & ½ tsp pepper and mix

5th Step

Heat the remainder of the oil (2 tbsp) in a skillet of medium size for around 2 minutes . Add in the mixture with the egg and then cool for around 2 minutes (the edges should begin to sizzle & set). Transfer the skillet to the oven. Leave the contents to bake for between 18 & 20 minutes, and ensure the center area is barely set. Take the skillet off the oven and leave it a minimum of 5 minutes to rest. Serve the chive crème fraiche alongside the dish . Sprinkle the dish with additional herbs if you wish.

Nutrition per Single Serving

305 cal/12g protein/5g carbohydrates/2g fiber/1.5g sugar (none added)/26.5g fat (8g saturated)/299mg cholesterol/377mg sodium

BRUSCHETTA WITH NECTARINE

INGREDIENTS: (2 SERVINGS)

White wine vinegar – 1½ tbsp

Honey – 1 tsp

Nectarine (in slices) – 1

Olive oil – ¼ cup

Black pepper (roughly cracked) – 2 tsp

Ricotta cheese (fresh) – 1/3 cup

Bread slices – 2

METHOD OF PREPARATION: (TOTAL TIME TAKEN: 15 MINUTES)

1st Step

Pour the vinegar & honey into a bowl and whisk. Add in the honey & continue whisking until it is well dissolved. Add in the nectarine; then toss to ensure it is properly coated. Leave contents for 10 min to ensure effective marination. Add in the olive oil plus the black pepper & toss

2nd Step

Take the ricotta & spread it onto the bread slices after grilling or toasting them. Scoop the mixture of nectarine and the juices and pour it on top; then serve.

Nutrition per Single Serving

484 calories/9g protein/35g carbs/3g fiber/9.5g sugar (3g added)/35g fat (7.5g saturated)/21mg cholesterol/304mg sodium.

BANANA-BLUEBERRY SMOOTHIE

INGREDIENTS: (2 SERVINGS)

Ripe bananas (big, peeled, chopped & frozen) – 2

Blueberries (frozen) – 1 cup (140g)

Milk – 1 cup (250ml)

Peanut butter (but optional) – 2 tbsp

Dates (but optional) – 2

METHOD OF PREPARATION: (TOTAL TIME TAKEN: 5 MINUTES)

Put the ingredients in a strong blender . Process until contents become smooth. Add milk according to the texture you prefer

Serve with toppings of your choice, e.g. blueberries or nuts.

Nutrition per Single Serving

261 cal/3.6g protein/41.6g carbs/10.4g fat (2g saturated)/23.1g sugars/6.3g fiber/165mg sodium

NB:

You can use water or fresh fruit juice in place of milk.

OMELETTE WITH CHEESE & AVOCADO

INGREDIENTS: (2 SERVINGS)

Olive oil – 1 tsp

Red onion (tiny & properly chopped) – 1

Kosher salt – as needed

Pepper – as needed

Cremini mushrooms (in slices) – 6

Baby spinach – 1 cup

Eggs – 4

Egg whites – 2

Cheddar cheese (roughly grated) – 2 ounces

Grape tomatoes (in halves) – 1 cup

Parsley (fresh & chopped) – ¼ cup

Avocado (tiny) – ½

METHOD OF PREPARATION: (TOTAL TIME TAKEN: 15 MINUTES)

1st Step

Put a skillet over medium heat and pour in the oil. Add in the onions, ¼ tsp salt & ¼ tsp pepper. Stir as you cook for around 4 min. Add in the mushrooms and continue to cook while stirring occasionally (mushrooms should become tender). Add in the spinach and stir. Continue to cook to ensure the spinach begins to wilt.

2nd Step

Add in the eggs and cook for a minute longer as you stir. Allow to cook further for between 2 & 3 minutes; and this time do not stir (the edges should become brown). Sprinkle the cheese on top and then fold in half to form some semi-circle.

3rd Step

Mix the tomatoes and the parsley plus the avocado by tossing. Use a spoon to scoop the mixture and spread over the omelette. Serve your breakfast.

Nutrition per Single Serving

350 cal/32g protein/10g carbs/10g fiber/7g sugar (none added)/22g fat (8g saturated)/200mg cholesterol/300mg sodium.

VEGETABLE MIX & SWEET POTATOES

INGREDIENTS: (2 SERVINGS)

Sweet potato (peeled & cut into cubes) – 1 (around 8 oz)

Beet (peeled & cut into cubes) – 1 (around 7 oz)

Brussels sprouts (cut into halves) – 20

Olive oil – 1 tbsp

Rosemary (fresh & well chopped) – 1 tsp

Salt – 1½ tsp

Pepper – ¼ tsp

Onion (well chopped) – ½

Garlic (well chopped) – 2 cloves

Mustard – 1 tbsp

Eggs (fried) – optional

METHOD OF PREPARATION: (TOTAL TIME TAKEN: 40 MINUTES)

1st Step

Pre-heat your oven up to 400°F. Take the vegetables and spread them out on some big baking sheet. Take ½ tbsp olive oil and drizzle it onto the vegetables. Next sprinkle on them the rosemary, a tsp salt & the pepper. Toss the contents well.

2nd Step

Begin roasting the vegetables and continue for between 20 & 25 min (they should become tender yet crispy on their outer side. In a big sauté pan, heat ½ tbsp oil on medium around 10 min before the vegetables are ready. Put onions into the hot oil and add ½ tsp salt. Leave contents to cook for between 4 & 5 min (the onions should be soft & with a little brownish). Throw the garlic onto the contents and continue to cook for an additional minute.

3rd Step

Take the ready vegetables and add them into the pan. Add also the mustard and stir the contents. Serve the vegetables in bowls. If you desire, place a fried egg on top.

Nutrition per Single Serving

312 calories/8.1 g fat/8.8 g protein/57.1 g carbs/11.4 g fiber/12.2 g sugar/1947 mg sodium

BANANA-WHOLE WHEAT PANCAKES

INGREDIENTS: (2 SERVINGS)

Whole wheat flour – 1 cup (120g)

Cane sugar (brown) – 2 tbsp

Baking powder – 2 tsp

Cinnamon (ground) – 1 tsp

Salt – 1/8 tsp

Milk (200ml) – ¾ cup

Flax egg – 1

Ripe banana (big & mashed) – ½ cup (120g)

Vanilla extract (optional) – ½ tsp

Cooking oil – for pancakes (optional)

METHOD OF PREPARATION: (TOTAL TIME TAKEN: 10 MINUTES)

Put the flour and baking powder into a big bowl. Add in the sugar, salt & cinnamon and mix everything well. Add in the milk and stir. Add in the egg, banana & vanilla extract and continue to stir so that the ingredients are evenly distributed. Scoop ¼ cup of the batter (around 65ml) and pour onto a hot pan that is lightly oiled. Cook for around 2 min on either side (color should become golden brown). Note it is time to flip the cake if bubbles have begun to emerge on the upper surface.. Serve

Nutrition per Single Serving

88 cal/3.1g protein/17.7g carbs/5g sugars/1.3g fat (0.1g saturated)/3g fiber/39mg sodium

COCONUT MILK YOGURT

INGREDIENTS: (4 SERVINGS)

Coconut milk (with all its fat) – 1 refrigerated can (400 ml)

Probiotics (in form of supplements)

METHOD OF PREPARATION: (TOTAL TIME TAKEN: 5 MINUTES)

Scoop out the top cream and put it in a bowl.Add in the powder from the probiotic supplement capsules. Mix the contents properly. Use a napkin or some cloth to cover the bowl . Put the bowl in a place that is cool & dark and let it remain for a minimum of 12hrs. Add some sweetener if you wish. Stir and then serve..

Nutrition per Single Serving

203 cal/1.7g protein/3.9g carbs/1.7g sugars/20.3g fat (18.6g saturated)/45mg sodium

NB:

You may serve the yoghurt with some toppings such as chopped or even baked apples.. You may use 2 tbsp of yoghurt bought from a store in case you do not have probiotic supplements.. The nutritional value is not exactly accurate considering water from the yoghurt has not been utilized in the recipe.

CAULIFLOWER & STRAWBERRY SMOOTHIE

INGREDIENTS: (2 SERVINGS)

Cauliflower (frozen) – 1 cup

Strawberries (frozen) – 1 cup

Banana (frozen) – 1

Almond milk (unsweetened) – 1¾ cup

Almond butter – 1 tbsp

Avocado – ½

Honey – 2 tsp

METHOD OF PREPARATION: (TOTAL TIME TAKEN: 8 MINUTES)

Take all the ingredients and blend them on high power (mixture should become smooth). Serve in glasses while garnishing as per personal preference.

Nutrition per Single Serving

244 cal/5g protein/34g carbs/12g fat/19g sugars/9g fiber/179mg sodium

MILKY PUMPKIN BREAD

INGREDIENTS: (10 SERVINGS)

Soy milk (unsweetened) – ½ cup

Lemon juice – 1 tbsp

Flour (all purpose) – 2 cups (250g)

Brown sugar – 1 cup (200g)

Baking powder – 1 tbsp

Cinnamon – 2 tsp

Salt – ¼ tsp

Pumpkin puree – 1½ cups (425g)

Canola oil – 1/3 cup (80ml)

Vanilla extract – 1 tsp

METHOD OF PREPARATION: (TOTAL TIME TAKEN: 70 MINUTES)

1st Step

Pre-heat oven up to 350°F. Spread parchment paper of size 9" by 5" on a loaf pan. Take the milk plus the lemon juice and mix them in some jar. Leave the mixture to rest for a minimum of 5 min at room temperature (the milk should the thick & curdled)

2nd Step

Put the flour, baking powder and sugar into a big bowl. Add in the salt & spice and mix properly. Add in the puree, vanilla extract & the oil and stir. Also, add in the mixture with milk and stir properly

3rd Step

Pour the batter onto a pan . Bake for between 50 & 60 min. Leave the milky pumpkin bread for around 15 min so that it cools. Transfer that bread onto some rack to cool properly.. Serve the bread with some healthy beverage, such as ginger tea.

Nutrition per Single Serving

260 cal/3.5g protein/44.1g carbs/21.5g sugar/8.2g fat (0.7g saturated)/2.1g fiber/74mg sodium

NB:

To check if the bread is properly done, pierce it with some toothpick at the center. In case the toothpick does not come out clean, cover the top of the bread with some foil so that that center can be done.. You can substitute a dish for the cooking rack

VEGAN MILKY BANANA MUFFINS

INGREDIENTS: (14 SERVINGS)

Soy milk (unsweetened) – ½ cup (120ml)

Apple cider vinegar – 2 tbsp

Flour (all purpose) – 1¾ cups (220g)

Granulated sugar – ¾ cup (150g)

Baking powder – 2½ tsp

Cinnamon (ground) – 1 tsp

Salt – ¼ tsp

Ripe bananas (medium) – 3 (11/3 cups/300g when mashed)

Canola oil – 1/3 cup (80ml)

Vanilla extract – 1 tsp

Chocolate chips (optional) – ¾ cup (130g)

METHOD OF PREPARATION: (TOTAL TIME TAKEN: 30 MINUTES)

1st Step

Pre-heat the oven up to 400° F. Spread 14 paper liners on an ordinary muffin tin

2nd Step

Put the milk & the vinegar in a bowl and mix them well. Leave the mixture still for 5 min (the milk should now be thick and curdled). Put in a large bowl the flour & sugar, salt, baking soda & baking powder, and cinnamon; then mix properly.. Add in the bananas in their mashed state, the oil and vanilla. Next add the milk plus the vinegar, and stir properly to ensure even distribution of ingredients. Add in the chocolate chips & continue to stir until everything is properly combined. Use a spoon to scoop out the batter; putting it in the liners (fill to the brim)

3rd Step

Bake the contents for between 20 & 30 min (batter should have turned a golden brown & the toothpick clean after piercing the middle)

4th Step

Take the pan out of the oven & let the muffins cool from a rack. Serve the muffins.

Nutrition per Single Serving

206 cal/2.6g protein/32.6g carbs/7.7g fat (1.6g Saturated)/18.1g sugar/1.7g fiber/50mg sodium

GARLICKY QUICHE

INGREDIENTS: (8 SERVINGS)

Vegan pie crust – 1

Extra virgin olive oil – 2 tbsp

Garlic (sliced) – 2 cloves

Onion (finely cut)– ½

Mushroom (in fine slices) – 2 cups (150g)

Cherry tomatoes (in halves) – 1 cup (180g)

Baby spinach (fresh) – 3 cups (90g)

Tofu (firm & drained) – 400g

Yeast – 2 tbsp

Soy milk (unsweetened) – 2 tbsp

Cornstarch – 1 tbsp

Black pepper (ground) – ½ tsp

Salt – ½ tsp

Black salt – ½ tsp

Turmeric (ground) – ¼ tsp

METHOD OF PREPARATION: (TOTAL TIME TAKEN: 50 MINUTES)

1st Step

Pre-heat oven up to 400°F. Pour the oil into a big skillet and heat it on medium. Add in the garlic & the onion and let them cook until they begin to turn golden brown. Add in the mushrooms & tomatoes and continue to cook (mushroom should become golden brown). Add in the spinach & let it cook to wilt. Take the skillet off the heat.

2nd Step

Put the tofu, yeast, milk, pepper & cornstarch, salt & black salt plus the tumeric into a food processor. Blend properly and then set the contents aside.

3rd Step

Line a pie pan with the crust. Pour onto it the blended contents . Take half of the ready vegetables and spread them over the crust at the bottom. Take the mixture with tofu & pour it over the vegetables. Next, drop on top the remainder of the vegetables.

4rth Step

Bake contents for between 35 & 45 min (the quiche should be firm and with golden color at the top). Take the pan off the oven and leave it for around 15 min (it should be cool a bit before you can proceed to slice the quiche). Serve either or even warm as per your preference.

Nutrition per Single Serving

321 cal/10.9g protein/25.3g carbs/2.3g sugar/20.3g fat (12.4g saturated)/2.7g fiber/242.9g sodium

INSTANT OATMEAL

INGREDIENTS: (4 SERVINGS)

Oats (rolled) – 1 cup (80g)

Soy milk (unsweetened) – 2½ cups (600ml)

Toppings (if preferred)

Fruit (fresh, dried or even frozen)

Nuts

Peanut butter

Maple syrup

Cinnamon (ground)

Cocoa (in powder form)

Applesauce

Berry compote

METHOD OF PREPARATION: (TOTAL TIME TAKEN: 55 MINUTES)

1st Step

Put the oats in an instant pot . Add in the milk and stir. Cover pot with a lid and align the valve with the 'sealing' mark or position. Press the button marked for pressure cooking while setting pressure at high. Leave contents to cook for two minutes

2nd step

Allow a 10-min natural release of pressure . Adjust the valve to align with 'venting' mark or position. Allow pressure release to complete properly.

3rd Step

Take the lid off the pot . Serve the dish (and add toppings if so preferred).

Nutrition per Single Serving

160 cal/7.7g protein/23.3g carbs/4g fat (0.5g saturated/6.4g sugars/3g fiber/80mg sodium

CAULIFLOWER-BASED SMOOTHIE

INGREDIENTS: (2 SERVINGS)

Peach (ripe, peeled & chopped) – 1 fruit

Mango (ripe, peeled & chopped) – 1 fruit

Carrots (big, peeled & chopped) – 2

Lime juice – 2½ tsp

Milk (unsweetened) – ½ cup

Spinach (optional)

METHOD OF PREPARATION: (TOTAL TIME TAKEN: 7 MINUTES)

Put all the ingredients into a food processor (a blender can also do). Process until the mixture becomes smooth (the mixture should be thick but drinkable by straw). If too thick, add milk a tbsp at a time.. Serve the ready smoothie.

Nutrition per Single Serving

170 cal/40g carbs/3g protein/2g fat (0.2g saturated)/33g sugars/6g fiber/96mg sodium/90mg calcium/0.9mg iron/702mg potassium

CHIA & PUMPKIN SEEDS GRANOLA

INGREDIENTS: (6 SERVINGS)

Oats (rolled) – 2 cups

Walnuts (chopped) – ½ cup

Pumpkin seeds – 1/3 cup

Chia seeds – ¼ cup

Pumpkin puree – 1/3 cup

Maple syrup – ½ cup

Pumpkin spice – 1 tsp

Nutmeg – ½ tsp

Ginger – ¼ tsp

Coconut oil – 2 tbsp

Sea salt – 1 tsp

Cranberries (dried) – 1/3 cup

METHOD OF PREPARATION: (TOTAL TIME TAKEN: 25 MINUTES)

1st Step

Pre-heat oven up to 325°F. Line aluminum foil on some baking sheet; then apply cooking spray on it

2nd Step

Put the oats and almonds in a big bowl. Add in the pepitas and walnuts as well as the pumpkin puree and the maple syrup. Next add in the vanilla extract, the pumpkin spice and the nutmeg. Finally, add in the ginger oil plus the sea salt. Mix the ingredients properly

3rd Step

Take the mixture with the oats and spread it on your baking sheet. Leave it to bake for around 15 min. Use a spatula to mix the contents . Return content to the oven and leave to bake for further 15 min (By now the dish should be golden brown and also crisp) . Wait for the dish to cool and then add in your cranberries as well as the chia seeds; then serve.

Nutrition per Single Serving

404 cal/10g protein/55g carbs/9g fiber/26g sugars/17g fat (3g saturated)/225mg sodium

CHEESY CHIA SEED MEATBALLS

INGREDIENTS: (7 SERVINGS)

Beef (ground) – 1½ pounds

Romano cheese (grated) – ½ cup

Chia seeds (raw & ground) – ¼ cup

Garlic (granulated) – 1 tsp

Italian parsley (fresh & well chopped) – ¼ cup

Egg (beaten) – 1

Oregano (dried) – 1 tsp

Worcestershire sauce – 2 tsp

Olive oil – 4 tsp (to use in frying)

METHOD OF PREPARATION: (TOTAL TIME TAKEN: 25 MINUTES)

1st Step

When the meat is at room temperature, sprinkle it with garlic, chia seeds & the oregano. Sprinkle it too with the parsley & cheese

2nd Step

Put the egg plus the Worcestershire sauce into a bowl; then mix

3rd Step

Take the mixture with meat and create meatballs of the same size (for this, roll the mixture in between your own hands). Pour 3 tsp olive oil into a big frying pan that is non-stick (4th tsp to be added later if required). Fry the meatballs over heat of medium level for around 15min, while turning them after every couple of minutes.

Nutrition per Single Serving

260 cal/24g protein/4g carbs/14g fat/4g fiber

FRUITY CHIA SEED POPS

INGREDIENTS: (10 SERVINGS)

Fresh fruit (your choice) – 1½ pounds

Chia seeds (ground) – 2 tbsp

Mint (fresh) – ½ ounce

Honey – 2 tbsp

Coconut water – ½ cup

Ice – ½ cup

METHOD OF PREPARATION: (TOTAL TIME TAKEN:10 MINUTES)

Put all the ingredients into some blender. Process until the mixture becomes smooth. Pour content into molds of ice pops Pierce the molds with sticks for ice pops. Put these ice pop molds into the fridge and leave them to freeze. Serve when they are firmly frozen.

Nutrition per Single Serving

36 cal/5g protein/7g carbs/1g fat/2g fiber

VEGAN DIP WITH FETA

INGREDIENTS: (18 SERVINGS)

Green peas (frozen then thawed) – ½ pound

Fresh asparagus – ½ pound

Chickpeas (rinsed & drained) – 8oz

Spinach leaves – 1 cup

Feta cheese (crumbled) – 1 cup

Lemon juice (fresh) – 1 tsp

White chia seeds – 3 tsp

Avocado oil (if you wish) – 1 tbsp

Sea salt (as needed for taste)

Pepper (as desired for taste)

METHOD OF PREPARATION: (TOTAL TIME TAKEN: 10 MINUTES)

Put all your ingredients into some food processor. Check to confirm proper seasoning (if need be put additional salt and/or pepper; and even lemon juice). Serve the mixture after sprinkling it with chia seeds plus the feta.

Nutrition per Single Serving

54 cal/4g protein/6g carbs/2.8g fat/2g fiber

OATS & GREENS SMOOTHIE

INGREDIENTS: (1 SERVINGS)

Banana (big one) – 1

Spinach (fresh) – 1 cup (30g)

Milk – ¾ cup (200ml)

Rolled oat – 2 tbsp

Dates (optional & pitted) – 2

METHOD OF PREPARATION: (TOTAL TIME TAKEN: 5 MINUTES)

Put the ingredients in a blender. Process until the mixture becomes smooth; then serve.

Nutrition per Single Serving

219 cal/8.9g protein/41.2g carbs/18.4g sugars/3.9g fat (0.7g saturated)/6g fiber/78mg sodium

KALE-BANANA SMOOTHIE

INGREDIENTS: (1 SERVINGS)

Kale – 1 cup (16g) – 1 cup

Banana (big) – 1

Milk – ¾ cup

Almond butter (but optional) – 1 tbsp

Cinnamon (but optional) – ½ tsp

Dates (but optional) – ½ tsp

METHOD OF PREPARATION: (TOTAL TIME TAKEN: 5 MINUTES)

Put the ingredients in a blender . Process until the mixture is smooth; then serve.

Nutrition per Single Serving

244 cal/6g protein/34.1g carbs/12g fat (1.1g saturated)/15.2 sugars/6.3g fiber/144mg sodium

CHAPTER 5:

36 MEDITERRANEAN LUNCH RECIPES

LETTUCE CHICKPEAS WRAPS

INGREDIENTS: (4 SERVINGS)

Tahini – ¼ cup

Extra virgin olive oil – ¼ cup

Lemon zest – 1tsp

Lemon juice – ¼ cup

Maple syrup (pure) – 1½ tsp

Kosher salt – ¾ tsp

Paprika – ½ tsp

Chickpeas (rinsed & saltless) – 2 cans (@15oz)

Red pepper (roasted & in slices) – ½ cup

Shallots (finely sliced) – ½ cup

Big leaves of Bibb lettuce – 12

Almonds (toasted & chopped) – ¼ cup

Parsley (fresh & chopped) – 2 tbsp

METHOD OF PREPARATION: (TOTAL TIME TAKEN: 10 MINUTES)

1st Step

In a big bowl, put in the tahini, paprika and lemon zest. Add in the lemon juice and maple syrup, as well as the salt and the oil. Whisk them well. Add in the shallots, chickpeas and the peppers and toss the contents

2nd Step

Scoop the mixture and dish it onto the lettuce leaves. Top the contents with the almonds plus the parsley. Wrap properly the leaves around their contents or filling; and proceed to serve.

Nutrition per Single Serving

498 cal/15.8 g protein/43.7 g carb/9.6 g fiber/4 g sugar (2 g added) /28 g fat (3.5 g saturated)/2232.6 IU Vitamin A/8.6 mg Vitamin C/62.2 mcg folate/162.5 mg calcium/4 mg iron/103.7 mg magnesium/620 mg potassium/567 mg sodium/0.4 g thiamin.

CHICKEN, CUCUMBER & QUINOA RECIPE

INGREDIENTS: (4 SERVINGS)

Chicken breasts (skinless, trimmed & boneless) – 1 lb

Salt – ¼ tsp

Pepper (ground) – ¼ tsp

Red pepper (rinsed & roasted) – 1 jar (7oz)

Almonds (in slivers) – ¼ cup

Extra virgin olive oil – 4 tbsp

Garlic (crushed) – 1 clove

Paprika – 1 tsp

Cumi.n (ground) – ½ tsp

Red pepper (crushed) – ¼ tsp (optional)

Quinoa (already cooked) – 2 cups

Kalamata olives (pitted & chopped) – ¼ cup

Red onion(nicely chopped)-¼ cup

Cucumber (sliced) – 1 cup

Feta cheese (crumbled) – ¼ cup

Parsley (fresh & nicely chopped) – 2 tbsp

METHOD OF PREPARATION: (TOTAL TIME TAKEN: 30 MINUTES)

1st Step

Place some rack within the upper 3rd part of the oven and pre-heat it on high. Spread foil on some baking sheet

2nd Step

Take the salt & the pepper and sprinkle them on the chicken. Place the chicken onto the baking sheet. Let the chicken broil and turn it only once, for between 14 & 18 min (thermometer should read 165°F). Remove the chicken from the baking sheet and place it onto some cutting board for slicing or shredding

3rd Step

Into a small food processor, put in the peppers, paprika and almonds. Add in the garlic, cumin & 2 tbsp oil. Process the contents until well pureed

4th Step

Mix the quinoa, the red onion, the remainder of 2 tbsp oil & olives in some bowl of medium size

5th Step

Distribute the mixture with quinoa among 4 separate bowls. Top the contents with an equal share of the cucumber, chicken & pepper sauce. Take the feta and the parsley and sprinkle them on dished contents.

Nutrition per Single Serving

519 cal/34.1 g protein/31.2 g carbs/4.2 g fiber/2.5 g sugar/26.9 fat(4.5 g saturated)/ 91.1 mg cholesterol/ 1158 IU Vitamin A/6.6 mg Vitamin C/62.5 mcg folate/113.1 mg calcium/2.8 mg iron/118.7 mg magnesium/685.7 mg potassium/683.5 mg sodium/0.3 mg thiamin.

PROSCIUTTO & HERBS

INGREDIENTS: (1 SERVINGS)

Prosciutto – 1 slice

Mozzarella – ½ stick

Breadsticks – 2 (in halves)

Dates – 2

Grapes – ½ cup

Radishes (big & halved) – 2

METHOD OF PREPARATION: (TOTAL TIME TAKEN: 5 MINUTES)

1st Step

Slice the prosciutto along its length. For every piece of cheese, wrap some slice all around it. In a container that is sealable, place in an orderly way the cheese and the breadsticks, the radishes, dates & the grapes . Refrigerate the dish until it is time to eat it.

Nutrition per Single Serving

452 cal/16.7 g protein/64.9 g carbs/4.2 g fiber/43.9 g sugar/18.1 g fat (5.9 g saturated)/26.1 mg cholesterol/347.6 IU Vitamin A/5.1mg Vitamin C/19.5 mcg folate/291 mg calcium/1.2 mg iron/45.8 mg magnesium/570.4 mg potassium/596.9 mg sodium/0.1 mg thiamin.

PITA-SALMON-WATERCRESS SANWICH

INGREDIENTS: (1 SERVINGS)

Yogurt (plain with no fat) – 2 tbsp

Dill (fresh & chopped) – 2 tbsp

Lemon juice – 2 tsp

Horseradish – ½tsp

Canned salmon (flaked & drained) – 3 oz

Pita bread (whole wheat, 6" diameter) – ½

Watercress – ½ cup

METHOD OF PREPARATION: (TOTAL TIME TAKEN: 10 MINUTES)

1st Step

Take yogurt, horseradish, the dill & lemon juice and put them into a tiny bowl. Add in the salmon and stir. Take the bread and stuff it with the salmon-based salad. Add watercress to the stuffing and serve.

Nutrition per Single Serving

239 cal/24.8 protein/19 g carbs/2.3 g fiber/3 g sugar/7.1 g fat (1.4 g saturated)/67.8 mg cholesterol/414.1 IU Vitamin A/8.2 mg Vitamin C/21.6 mcg folate/273.8 mg calcium/1.5 mg iron/54.7 mg magnesium/436.1 mg potassium/510.2 mg sodium/0.2 mg thiamin.

GREEK VEGETABLE-RICH MEATBALL

INGREDIENTS: (4 SERVINGS)

Spinach (frozen, thawed & chopped) – 1 cup

Turkey (lean & ground) – 1 lb

Feta cheese (crumbled) – ½ cup

Garlic powder – ½ tsp

Oregano (dried) – ½ tsp

Salt – ½ tsp

Pepper (ground) – ½ tsp

Quinoa (cooked & cooled) – 2 cups

Lemon juice – 2 tbsp

Olive oil – 1 tbsp

Parsley (chopped) – ½ cup

Mint (chopped) – 3 tbsp

Cucumber (in slices) – 2 cups

Cherry tomatoes – 1 pint

Tzatziki – ¼ cup

METHOD OF PREPARATION: (TOTAL TIME TAKEN: 35 MINUTES)

1st Step

Squeeze out moisture from the spinach. Combine that spinach with the oregano, the garlic, feta & turkey. Add in the feta cheese, ¼ tsp salt & ¼ tsp pepper and mix properly. Create meatballs from that mixture; 12 in all

2nd Step

Take a big skillet (non-stick) and heat it on medium. Apply cooking spray on it. Take the meatballs and drop them into the pan in batches. Cook them for between 10 & 12 min (they should turn brown on every side & no pink should remain on their middle part. Thermometer reading should indicate 165°F). Leave the meatballs to cool.

3rd Step

Put the quinoa, the mint, the parsley & the lemon juice in a bowl of medium size and mix them. Add in the oil plus the remainder of the salt & pepper (¼ tsp each) and mix the contents. Take 4 containers and share the bowl contents equally among them. Top them with meatballs (3 for each container). Add to the topping ½ cup of cucumber plus ½ cup of cherry tomatoes.

4th Step

Cover the containers with their respective lids. Refrigerate them for a period of approximately 4 days. Divide the tzatziki by sharing it in 4 small containers.

5th Step

Take the meatballs and use a microwave to heat them using a container that is microwave-safe (meatballs should reach steaming point). Transfer the hot meatballs to their respective containers. Serve meatballs alongside the tzatziki.

Nutrition per Single Serving

392 cal/32.4 g protein/29.3 g carbs/5.6 g fiber/5.3 sugar/17.2 g fat (5.8 g saturated)/ 83.2 mg cholesterol/6153.2 IU Vitamin A/27.8 mg Vitamin C/135.5 mcg folate/207.6 mg calcium/5.5 mg iron/116 mg magnesium/919 mg potassium/542.5 mg sodium/0.2 mg thiamin.

LENTIL & CUCUMBER SALAD

INGREDIENTS: (6 SERVINGS)

Brown lentils (cooked) – 3 cups

Cherry tomatoes (in halves) – 1 pint

English Cucumber (chopped) – 1½ cups

Kalamata olives (roughly chopped & pitted) – ½ cup

Red onion (in thin slices) – ½ cup

Feta cheese (crumbled) – ½ cup

Salt – ½ tsp

Pepper (ground) – ½ tsp

Red wine vinegar – 3 tbsp

Shallot (nicely chopped) – 1 tbsp

Garlic (minced) – ½ tsp

Honey – ½ tsp

Extra virgin olive oil – ¼ cup

METHOD OF PREPARATION: (TOTAL TIME TAKEN: 15 MINUTES)

1st Step

Take the lentils, the tomatoes & the cucumber and put them into a big bowl. Add in the olives and the onions, as well as the feta cheese. Finally add ¼ tsp salt plus ¼ tsp pepper and mix the contents well. Set the mixture aside.

2nd Step

Take the vinegar, the shallot & the garlic and pour them into a tiny bowl. Take ¼ tsp salt plus ¼ tsp pepper and add into the same bowl. Whisk the contents to have them mix well. Add in the oil as you continue the whisking

3rd Step

Take the dressing and pour it into mixture with the lentils; and mix contents gently. Proceed to serve.

Nutrition per Single Serving

271 cal/11 g protein/25 g carbs/15 g fat (3 g saturated)/8 mg cholesterol/5 g sugar/490 IU Vitamin A/476 mg sodium/8 g fiber/528 mg potassium/1 mg equivalents to niacin.

QUINOA, NUTS & FETA SALAD WITH CHERRY TOMATOES

INGREDIENTS: (6 SERVINGS)

Quinoa (cooked & cooled) – 4 cups

Pine nuts (toasted) – ¼ cup

Feta cheese (crumbled) – ¾ cup

Red wine vinegar – 3 tbsp

Oregano (fresh & chopped) – 1 tbsp

Garlic (minced) – 1 clove

Cherry tomatoes (in halves) – 2 cups

Red bell pepper (medium & chopped in pc 1" thick) – 1

Red onion (in slices) – 1 cup

Kalamata olives (pitted) – ¼ cup

Salt – ¼ tsp

Extra virgin olive oil – ¼ cup

Pepper (ground) – ½ tsp

Basil (fresh & chopped) – for garnishing if preferred

METHOD OF PREPARATION: (TOTAL TIME TAKEN: 25 MINUTES)

1st Step

Pre-heat the oven and ensure the rack is 6" away from the source of the heat. Take the vinegar, the garlic and the oregano and put them into a tiny bowl. Add in the salt, ¼ tsp pepper & 3 tbsp oil. Whisk all the bowl contents.

2nd Step

Take the tomatoes, the olives and the bell pepper, and put them into a big bowl. Add in ¼ tsp pepper plus the remainder of the oil (1 tbsp). Toss the contents well. Take a baking sheet and spread it evenly within the oven. Put in the vegetables and broil them for between 8 & 10 min (the vegetables should be a little charred but tender); ensuring to stir halfway the cooking Transfer the ready vegetables onto a big bowl while discarding the juices on the pan.

3rd Step

Onto the ready vegetables, add the quinoa and the feta, plus the pine nuts. Take the vinaigrette and drizzle it on the contents. Toss the bowl to ensure proper coating. Garnish the dish with basil as you like.

Nutrition per Single Serving

359 cal/9 g protein/34 g carbs/21 g fat (4 g saturated)/13 mg cholesterol/5 g sugar/5 g fiber/1117 IU Vitamin A/421 mg sodium/1 mg equivalents of niacin.

CHICKPEAS & RED PEPPER SOUP

INGREDIENTS: (2:SERVINGS)

Red pepper soup (low in sodium & roasted) – 1 carton (32 oz)

Chickpeas (rinsed & unsalted) – 1 can (15 oz)

Baby spinach – 3 cups

METHOD OF PREPARATION: (TOTAL TIME TAKEN: 45 MINUTES)

1st Step

Put the red pepper soup into a saucepan of medium size and heat it on medium until it begins to simmer

2nd Step

Add in the chickpeas plus the baby spinach. Let the simmering continue for around a minute for the spinach to wilt

Serve .

Nutrition per Single Serving

488 cal/26 g protein/78 g carbs/8 g fat/20 mg cholesterol/30 g sugar/15 g fiber/5500 IU Vitamin A/778 mg sodium

BROCCOLI, KALE, BEANS & YOGURT

INGREDIENTS: (1 SERVINGS)

Slaw mix of kale & broccoli – 1 bag (10 oz)   Yogurt – ¼ cup

Cannellini beans (rinsed & unsalted) – 1 can
(15 oz)

METHOD OF PREPARATION: (TOTAL TIME TAKEN: 5 MINUTES)

1st Step

Mix the beans & the slaw mix

2nd Step

Add in the dressing Toss the contents to ensure even distribution and coating.

Nutrition per Single Serving

362 cal/14 g protein/40 g carbs/7 g sugar/15 g fat/12 mg cholesterol/12 g fiber/2931 IU Vitamin A/372 mg sodium

FRUIT & VEGETABLE SALAD WITH FETA CHEESE & WALNUTS

INGREDIENTS: (4 SERVINGS)

Extra virgin olive oil – 1½ tbsp

Balsamic vinegar – 1 tbsp

Shallot (nicely chopped) – 2 tsp

Salt – ¼ tsp

Pepper (ground) – ¼ tsp

Baby spinach – 6 cups

Strawberries (nicely sliced) – 1 cup

Feta cheese (crumbled) – ¼ cup

Walnuts (toasted & chopped) – ¼ cup

METHOD OF PREPARATION: (TOTAL TIME TAKEN: 15 MINUTES)

1st Step

Put the vinegar and the shallot into a big bowl. Add in the salt plus the pepper and whisk the contents. Leave the bowl still for between 5 & 10 min, to let the shallots become soft & a little mellow

2nd Step

Into the same bowl, add in the spinach and the strawberries. Also add in the feta cheese & the walnuts. Toss contents to ensure the dressing is well distributed.

Nutrition per Single Serving

158 cal/4.8 g protein/8.6 g carbs/12.1 fat(2.6 g saturated)/3.3 g sugar/8.3 mg cholesterol/3.4 g fiber/5566 IU Vitamin A/48.6 mg Vitamin C/20.7 mcg folate/142.4 mg calcium/3.2 mg iron/79.8 mg magnesium/113.5 mg potassium/298 mg sodium/0.1 mg thiamin.

KALE, COUSCOUS & BASIL VINAIGRETTE

INGREDIENTS: (1 SERVINGS)

Kale (well chopped) – 1 cup

Couscous (whole wheat) – ¼ cup

Canned chickpeas (rinsed) – 2/3rd cup

Basil vinaigrette – 4 tbsp

METHOD OF PREPARATION: (TOTAL TIME TAKEN: 5 MINUTES)

Put the kale, the chickpeas & the couscous in some medium-size bowl

Mix well and serve.

Nutrition per Single Serving

481 cal/17.3 g protein/67.6 g carbs/13.4 g fiber/4.4 g sugar (3 g added)/16.7 g fat (2 g saturated)/1939.1 IU Vitamin A/20.6 mg Vitamin C/160 mcg folate/112.6 mg calcium/3.9 mg iron/66.6 mg magnesium/491.3 mg potassium/282.5 mg sodium/0.1 mg thiamin.

HUMMUS & GREEK SALAD WITH FETA CHEESE

INGREDIENTS: (1 SERVINGS)

Arugula – 2 cups

Cherry tomatoes (in halves) – 1/3 cup

Cucumber (in slices) – 1/3 cup

Red onion (chopped) – 1 tbsp

Extra virgin olive oil – 1½ tbsp

Red wine vinegar – 2 tsp

Pepper (ground) – a pinch

Feta cheese – 1 tbsp

Pita (whole wheat) – 1 (4" diameter)

Hummus – ¼ cup

METHOD OF PREPARATION: (TOTAL TIME TAKEN: MINUTES)

1st Step

Put the arugula and the tomatoes in some bowl. Add in the cucumber, the onion and the pepper, as well as the vinegar and the oil. Top the contents with the feta cheese. Serve the dish alongside hummus and the pita.

Nutrition per Single Serving

422 cal/10.9 g protein/30.5 carbs/7.3 g fiber/4.3 g sugar/29.9 g fat (5.3 g saturated)/8.3 mg cholesterol/1456.6 IU Vitamin A/15 mg Vitamin C/119.1 mcg folate/153.5 mg calcium/3.3 mg iron/96.9 mg magnesium/543.8 mg potassium/485.8 mg sodium.

PROSCIUTTO, BAGUETTE & MOZZARELLA BALLS WITH STRAWBERRY

INGREDIENTS: (2 SERVINGS)

Cantaloupe (in cubes) – 1 cup

Prosciutto (in halves of slices) – 6 slices (thin)

Mozzarella balls (tiny & fresh) – 10

Cherry tomato (in halves) – ½ cup

Baguette (whole wheat) – 6 slices (¼" thick)

Hazelnuts (unsalted) – ½ cup

Strawberries (dipped in chocolate) – 4

METHOD OF PREPARATION: (TOTAL TIME TAKEN: 20 MINUTES)

Arrange all the ingredients neatly and equally on 2 large plates. Serve.

Nutrition per Single Serving

546 cal/24 g protein/44 g carbs/6.5 g fiber/16.4 g sugar (6 g added)/33.8 g fat (9.7 g saturated)/52.1 mg cholesterol/3391.4 IU Vitamin A/54 mg Vitamin C/318.1 mg calcium/3 mg iron/66.2 mg magnesium/555.8 mg potassium/936 mg sodium/0.2 mg thiamin/53.4 mcg folate.

MEDITERRANEAN-TYPE WRAPS

INGREDIENTS: (4 SERVINGS)

Water – ½ cup

Couscous (whole wheat) – 1/3 cup

Parsley (fresh & chopped) – 1 cup

Mint (fresh & chopped) – ½ cup

Lemon juice – ¼ cup

Extra virgin olive oil – 3 tbsp

Garlic (minced) – 2 tsp

Salt – ¼ tsp

Pepper (just ground) – ¼ tsp

Chicken tenders – 1 lb

Tomato (chopped) – 1 (medium size)

Cucumber (chopped) – 1 cup

Spinach Wraps (10" thick) – 4

METHOD OF PREPARATION: (TOTAL TIME TAKEN: 40 MINUTES)

1st Step

Boil water in a tiny saucepan. Pour in the couscous and stir. Remove the pan from the heat, cover the contents, and leave them still for around 5 min. Use a fork to fluff the contents

2nd Step

Put the parsley and the mint into another tiny bowl. Add in the garlic and the lemon juice as well as the oil. Finally add in 1/8 tsp salt plus 1/8 tsp pepper.

3rd Step

Put the chicken tenders in a bowl of medium size . Add in 1 tbsp of the mixture with parsley. Next add in the 1/8 salt remaining and toss the contents

4th Step

Put the tenders into a big skillet (non-stick). Cook the tenders on medium heat for between 3 & 5 min on every side. Transfer the ready tenders onto some cutting board and cut them into pieces of bite size once sufficiently cool

5th Step

Take the remainder of the mixture with parsley and add it to the couscous. Add in the tomato plus the cucumber as well and stir the contents.

6th Step

Scoop ¾ cup couscous mixture and spread it onto the wraps. Share the chicken among all the wraps. Embark on rolling up the wraps as you tuck in their sides, so that they resemble burritos (the contents/ingredients should be well held in). Slice into halves and serve.

Nutrition per Single Serving

510 cal/32.3 g protein/54.9 g carbs/5.7 g fiber/4.5 g sugar/17.9 g fat (3.3 g saturated)/62.7 mg cholesterol/2026.5 IU Vitamin A/32.8 mg Vitamin C/192 mcg folate/6.1 mg iron/564.2 mg potassium/165 mg calcium/59.1 mg magnesium/725.6 mg sodium/0.4 mg thiamin.

GRILLED TURKEY, PITA BREAD & GRAPES

INGREDIENTS: (1 SERVINGS)

Chickpeas (rinsed) – ¼ cup

Cucumber (diced) – ¼ cup

Tomato (diced) – ¼ cup

Olives (diced) – 1 tbsp

Feta cheese (crumbled) – 1 tbsp

Parsley (fresh & chopped) – 1 tbsp

Extra virgin olive oil – ½ tsp

Red wine vinegar – 1 tsp

Turkey breast (grilled) – 3 oz

Grapes – 1 cup

Pita bread (whole wheat) – 1 (cut into quarters)

Hummus – 2 tbsp

METHOD OF PREPARATION: (TOTAL TIME TAKEN: 15 MINUTES)

1st step

Put the chickpeas, vinegar, cucumber and the feta cheese into some bowl of medium size. Add in the tomato and parsley, as well as the olives & the oil; then mix everything. Transfer the contents into some medium-size container.

2nd Step

Put the grilled turkey into a container of medium size.

3rd Step

Pack the grapes in some tiny container

Do the same for the pita bread

Put the hummus into some container of dip-size.

Nutrition per Single Serving

497 cal/36.7 g protein/60.5 g carbs/7.9 g fiber/26.3 g sugar/13.8 g fat (2.9 g saturated)/76.4 mg cholesterol/888.5 IU Vitamin A/16.8 mg Vitamin C/79.6 mcg folate/115.9 mg calcium/3.7 mg iron/101.1 mg magnesium/837.9 mg potassium/697 mg sodium/0.3 mg thiamin.

CHICKEN & CUCUMBER STUFFED PITA WITH GREEK YOGURT

INGREDIENTS: (4 SERVINGS)

Lemon zest – 1 tsp

Lemon juice (fresh) – 2 tbsp

Olive oil – 5 tsp

Oregano (dried 1) – 1 tsp

Garlic (minced) – 2¾ tsp

Red pepper (crushed) – ¼ tsp

Chicken tender – 1 lb

English cucumber (halved & seeded; then grated) – 1

English cucumber (halved then sliced) – 1

Salt – ½ tsp

Greek yogurt (plain with no fat) – ¾ cup

Mint (fresh & chopped) – 2 tsp

Dill (fresh & chopped) – 2 tsp

Pepper (ground) – 1 tsp

Pita bread (whole wheat & in halves) – 2 (6.5" diameter)

Lettuce – 4 leaves

Red onion (in slices) – ½ cup

Plum tomatoes (chopped)– 1 cup

METHOD OF PREPARATION: (TOTAL TIME TAKEN: 105 MINUTES)

1st Step

Take the lemon zest and lemon juice and pour them into a big bowl. Add in 3 tbsp oil plus the oregano; 2 tsp of garlic & the red pepper. Add in the chicken then toss to ensure the chicken is well coated. Put the bowl in the refrigerator for a period between 1 & 4 hours so that the chicken can marinate.

2nd Step

Put the grated cucumber into some sieve of fine mesh. Add in ¼ tsp salt and toss to mix. Leave the contents for around 15 min to allow draining. Afterward, squeeze out the remaining moisture. Transfer the contents into a bowl of medium size. Add in the yogurt, the mint and the dill. Also, add in the ground pepper plus the remainder of the oil (2 tsp), garlic (¾ tsp) & salt (¼ tsp). Put the bowl into the refrigerator and leave it until it is time to serve the meal.

3rd Step

Pre-heat grill on medium high. Grill your chicken and give each side between 3 & 4 min (thermometer should read 165°F at the center of the chicken by the time the chicken is ready)

5th Step

As you serve the meal, spread a bit of sauce within each half of the pita. Then tuck in your ready chicken, the lettuce plus the red onion, as well as the tomatoes and the cucumber slices.

Nutrition per Single Serving

353 cal/37.5 g protein/33.3 g carb/5.8 g fiber/6.3 g sugar/8.6 g fat (0.9 g saturated)/57.7 mg cholesterol/1139.3 IU Vitamin A/15.1 mg Vitamin C/31.4 mcg folate/85.4 mg calcium/1.6 mg iron/53.9 mg magnesium/458.6 mg potassium/558.8 mg sodium.

SLOW COOKING CHICKEN THIGHS & PEAS WITH FRESH HERBS

INGREDIENTS: (6 SERVINGS)

Chickpeas (dry but soaked 12hrs earlier) – 1½ cups

Water – 4 cups

Yellow onion (nicely chopped) – 1 (big)

Tomatoes (unsalted & diced) – 1 can (15 oz)

Tomato paste – 2 tbsp

Garlic (nicely chopped) – 4 cloves

Bay leaf – 1

Cumin (ground) – 4 tsp

Paprika – 4 tsp

Cayenne pepper – ¼ tsp

Pepper (ground) – ¼ tsp

Chicken thighs (with bone, skinless & trimmed) – 2 lb

Artichoke hearts (drained then quartered) – 1 can (14 oz)

Olives (pitted & oil cured; also halved) – ¼ cup

Salt – ½ tsp

Parsley (fresh & chopped) – ¼ cup

METHOD OF PREPARATION: (TOTAL TIME TAKEN: 260 MINUTES)

1st Step

Drain the chickpeas, then put them into a big slow cooker. Add in the water, the onion and the tomatoes plus their juices. Also add in the tomato paste and the garlic, plus the bay leaf, cumin & paprika. Add in too the cayenne plus the ground pepper. Stir the contents to thoroughly combine them

2nd Step

Add the chicken to the chickpeas mixture and cook on low heat when covered for around 8 hrs.

3rd Step

Pick out the chicken and place it on some chopping board to cool a bit. Get rid of the bay leaf. Add in artichokes plus the olives. Add in the salt and proceed to stir the mixture.

4th Step

Embark on shredding the chicken and discard its bones. Throw the shredded chicken into the mixture with artichokes and stir.

5th Step

Serve your dish and top it with the parsley.

Nutrition per Single Serving

447 cal/33.6 g protein/43 g carbs/11.6 g fiber/15.3 g fat (3.3 g saturated)/8.5 g sugar/76.5 mg cholesterol/1590 IU Vitamin A/15.1 mg Vitamin C/194.1 mcg folate/114.7 mg calcium/5.7 mg iron/78.7 mg magnesium/608.8 mg potassium/761.8 mg sodium.

MEDITERRANEAN PASTA WITH HUMMUS & BABY KALE

INGREDIENTS: (1 SERVINGS)

Hummus (plain) – 2 tbsp

Water –l tbsp

Extra virgin olive oil – 2 tsp

Red bell pepper (chopped) – ½ cup

Artichoke hearts (sliced in halves & drained) – ½ cup

Baby kale (roughly packed) – 1 cup

Kalamata olives (pitted & chopped) – 4

Light tuna (drained & unsalted) – 1 can (3 oz)

Pasta (cooked; also whole wheat preferred) – ½ cup

Feta cheese (crumbled) – 1 tbsp

Walnuts (toasted & chopped) – 1 tbsp

Lemon juice (fresh) – ¼ lemon

METHOD OF PREPARATION: (TOTAL TIME TAKEN: 20 MINUTES)

1st Step

Pour the hummus and the water into a tiny bowl. Whisk contents and then set the bowl aside.

2nd Step

Pre-heat a skillet (non-stick) on medium heat. Add in the bell pepper and proceed to cook for a single minute. Add in artichoke hearts, olives & the kale

3rd Step

Add I the tuna without breaking the big pieces; and lightly stir contents. Cook for an additional minute, to ensure the tuna has become warm. Add in the pasta and stir. Take the skillet off the heat and pour in the hummus rich sauce. Toss the contents; then use the feta cheese plus the walnuts as topping. Take the lemon juice and drizzle over the contents. Meal is ready for serving.

Nutrition per Single Serving

506 cal/33.4 g protein/38.3 g carbs/7 g fiber/3.4 g sugar/24.5 g fat (4 g saturated)/33.9 mg cholesterol/3090.5 IU Vitamin A/75.1 mg Vitamin C/164.2 mcg folate/101.7 mg calcium/3.6 mg iron/97.5 mg magnesium/540.2 mg potassium/746.8 mg sodium.

PEPPERY QUINOA WITH CHICKPEA & ALMONDS

INGREDIENTS: (4SERVINGS)

Red pepper (rinsed & roasted) – 1 jar (7 oz)

Almonds (slivered) – ¼ cup

Extra virgin olive oil – 4 tbsp

Garlic (minced) – 1 clove (small-size)

Paprika – 1 tsp

Cumin (ground) – ½ tsp

Red pepper (crushed) – ¼ tsp (optional)

Quinoa (cooked) – 2 cups

Kalamata olives (chopped) – ¼ cup

Red onion (nicely chopped) – ¼ cup

Chickpeas (rinsed) – 1 can (15 oz)

Cucumber (diced) – 1 cup

Feta cheese (crumbled) – ¼ cup

Parsley (fresh & well chopped) – 2 tbsp

METHOD OF PREPARATION: (TOTAL TIME TAKEN: 20 MINUTES)

1st Step

Into a small food processor, put in the peppers, the almonds and the garlic. Add in the paprika & cumin, as well as 2 tbsp oil. Process the ingredients until the pureed content is reasonably smooth.

2nd Step

In a bowl of medium size, put in the quinoa, the olives and the red onion. Add in also the remainder of the oil (2 tbsp); then mix contents

3rd Step

Serve the meal by sharing the mixture with quinoa among some 4 bowls. Similarly, share the chickpeas equally as topping. Distribute the cucumber plus the pepper sauce in the same manner; as topping.. Finally, take the feta cheese & the parsley and sprinkle them over the dishes.

Nutrition per Single Serving

479 cal/12.7 g protein/49.5 g carbs/7.7 g fiber/2.5 g sugar/24.8 g fat (4.3 g saturated)/8.3 mg cholesterol/1145.8 IU Vitamin A/9.6 mg Vitamin C/105.8 mcg folate/135.8 mg calcium/3.5 mg iron/109.9 mg magnesium/442.6 mg potassium/646 mg sodium/0.2 mg thiamin.

MEDITERRANEAN SWEET PEPPERS, KALE AND LENTILS

INGREDIENTS: (4 SERVINGS)

Red wine vinegar – ¼ cup

Olive oil – 2 tbsp

Tomatoes (dried, finely sliced & not packed in oil) – 1 tbsp

Garlic (minced) – 1 clove

Mustard – ½ tsp

Salt – ¼ tsp

Black pepper – ¼ tsp

Baby kale (fresh) – 8 cups

Lentils (refrigerated then steamed) – 1 package (9 oz)

Red sweet pepper (chopped) – 1 cup

Parmesan cheese (shredded) – ¼ cup.

METHOD OF PREPARATION: (TOTAL TIME TAKEN: 15 MINUTES)

1st Step

Take a big serving bowl and put in the olive oil and vinegar. Add in the tomatoes and garlic, as well as the mustard, salt & the pepper. Whisk the ingredients and then add in kale and toss

2nd Step

Top the content of the serving bowl with the lentils plus the sweet pepper. Finally, sprinkle it with the cheese and serve.

Nutrition per Single Serving

186 cal/9.6 g protein/18.2 g carbs/7.4 g fiber/3.2 g sugar/8.6 g fat (1.8 g saturated)/3.6 mg cholesterol/3656.9 IU Vitamin A/49 mg Vitamin C/81.9 mcg folate/215.8 mg calcium/3.6 mg iron/10.4 mg magnesium/376.2 mg potassium/464.1 mg sodium.

TABBOULEH, HUMMUS, BERRIES WITH PITA BREAD

INGREDIENTS: (4 SERVINGS)

Tabbouleh – 2 cups

Beet hummus – 1 cup

Raspberries – 1 cup

Blackberries – 1 cup

Pita bread (whole wheat) – 4; each 4" in diameter

Snap peas (ends removed) – 1 cup

Radishes – 4

Mixed olives – 1 cup

Pistachios (roasted & unsalted) – 2/3 cup

Vegan cookies – 4

METHOD OF PREPARATION: (TOTAL TIME TAKEN: 15 MINUTES)

Distribute the ingredients among 4 big plates and serve.

Nutrition per Single Serving

537 cal/13.5 g protein/54.8 g carbs/14.1 g fiber/12.5 g sugar (3 g added)/31.2 g fat (4.9 g saturated)/2020.7 IU Vitamin A/59 mg Vitamin C/110.8 mcg folate/179.6 mg calcium/5.7 mg iron/128.7 mg magnesium/787.3 mg potassium/654.7 mg sodium/0.4 mg thiamin.

GARLIC-RICH CHEESE RAVIOLI & VEGETABLE BROTH

INGREDIENTS: (4 SERVINGS)

Extra virgin olive oil – 1 tbsp

Mix of Bell pepper & onions (thawed then diced) – 2 cups

Garlic (minced) – 2 cloves

Red pepper (crushed) – ¼ tsp

Tomatoes (crushed) – 1 can (15 oz)

Vegetable broth – 1 can (15 oz)

Hot water – 1½ cups

Basil (dried) – 1 tsp

Cheese ravioli – 1 package (between 6 & 9 oz)

Zucchini (diced) – 2 cups

Pepper (fresh & ground) – just enough to provide taste

METHOD OF PREPARATION: (TOTAL TIME TAKEN: 25 MINUTES)

1st Step

Put the oil in a big saucepan and heat on medium. Add in the mix of onion & pepper, the red pepper, plus the garlic. Stir contents and cook for a single minute.

2nd Step

Add in the tomatoes, the basil, plus the water and the broth. Keep cooking on high-level heat until boiling starts

3rd Step

Add in the ravioli and let contents continue cooking. The time for letting the ravioli cook should be less by 3 minutes that indicated on the package.. Add in the zucchini and let boiling continue for around 3 min (zucchini should become tender but crisp). Finally, use pepper to season the dish.

Nutrition per Single Serving

261 cal/10.6 g protein/32.6 g carbs/7 g fiber/11.8 g sugar/8.3 g fat (3 g saturated)/28.4 mg cholesterol/2278.7 IU Vitamin A/23.9 mg Vitamin C/16 mcg folate/97.4 mg calcium/5 mg iron/15 mg magnesium/731.9 mg potassium/354.4 mg sodium.

CHICKEN SALAD & GREEK YOGURT WITH PESTO

INGREDIENTS: (6 SERVINGS)

Greek yogurt (plain with no fat) – ½ cup

Mayonnaise – 1/3 cup

Shallot (minced) – 2 tbsp

Pesto – 2 tbsp

Lemon juice – 2 tsp

Salt – ½ tsp

Pepper (ground) – ½ tsp

Chicken (cooked & chopped) – 3 cups

Arugula (roughly chopped & packed) – 1 cup

Cherry tomatoes (in halves) – ½ cup

Pine nuts (toasted) – 3 tbsp

METHOD OF PREPARATION: (TOTAL TIME TAKEN: 20 MINUTES)

1st Step

In a big bowl, pour in the yogurt, the mayonnaise and the lemon juice. Add in the shallot and pesto, as well as the salt & pepper. Mix the ingredients so that they combine well.

2nd Step

Add in the chicken, the arugula, plus the tomatoes and stir. Finally, take the nuts and use them as topping. Serve the meal at your preferred temperature.

Nutrition per Single Serving

209 cal/13 g protein/3.4 g carbs/0.6 g fiber/1.5 g sugar/15.7 g fat (2.6 g saturated)/32.1 mg cholesterol/292.9 IU Vitamin A/3.6 mg Vitamin C/11.3 mcg folate/73.4 mg calcium/0.9 mg iron/28.5 mg magnesium/216.9 mg potassium/357.6 mg sodium/0.1 mg thiamin.

TUNA SALAD WITH SPINACH & ORANGE

INGREDIENTS: (1 SERVINGS)

Water – 1½ tbsp

Tahini – 1½ tbsp

Lemon juice – 1½ tbsp

Light tuna (chunks preserved in water; then drained) – 1 can (5 oz)

Kalamata olives (pitted & chopped) – 4

Feta cheese – 2 tbsp

Parsley – 2 tbsp

Baby spinach – 2 cups

Orange (medium & sliced) – 1

METHOD OF PREPARATION: (TOTAL TIME TAKEN: 10 MINUTES)

Put the water, the tahini and the lemon juice in some bowl. Add in the tuna, the feta & the parsley, as well as the olives. Whisk and stir to mix the salad ingredients properly. Serve the salad over the spinach, with the slices of orange on the side.

Nutrition per Single Serving

376 cal/25.7 g protein/26.2 g carbs/5.8 g fiber/13.9 g sugar/21 g fat (5.2 g saturated)/46.3 mg cholesterol/5920.2 IU Vitamin A/94 mg Vitamin C/154.1 mcg folate/271 mg calcium/4.8 mg iron/102.5 mg magnesium/779.8 mg potassium/664.8 mg sodium/0.6 mg thiamin.

CHICKEN SALAD WITH EDAMAME & FETA CHEESE

INGREDIENTS: (4 SERVINGS)

Chicken breast (skinless & boneless; also trimmed) – 8 oz

Red wine vinegar – ¼ cup

Extra virgin olive oil – 3 tbsp

Salt – ¼ tsp

Pepper (ground) – ¼ tsp

Edamame (frozen then thawed) – 8 oz

Romaine (chopped) – 8 cups

Cherry tomatoes (in halves) – 1 cup

European cucumber (in slices) – ½

Feta cheese (crumbled) – ½ cup

Basil (fresh & slivered) – ¼ cup

Kalamata olives (in slices) – ¼ cup

Red onion (slivered) – ¼ cup

METHOD OF PREPARATION: (TOTAL TIME TAKEN: 30 MINUTES)

1st Step

Put the chicken in a saucepan of medium size. Add in water ensuring it covers the chicken by around 2". Put the pan over a heat source to boil the chicken. Minimize the heat so that contents begin to simmer. Continue cooking for between 12 & 15 min; until the thermometer reading from the chicken's middle part is 165° F.

2nd Step

Take the chicken out of the pan and onto some cutting board. Let the chicken remain still for around 5 min, so that it cools. Chop the chicken into small pieces.

3rd Step

Put the vinegar and the oil into a big bowl. Add in the salt and the pepper. Add in the edamame, the romaine and the tomatoes. Also add in the cucumber, the olives, onion and basil. Finally, add in the feta cheese and the chicken; and toss the contents.

Nutrition per Single Serving

336 cal/22.3 g protein/14.2 g carbs/5.9 g fiber/5.1 g sugar/21.6 g fat (5.4 g saturated)/48 mg cholesterol/8994.2 IU Vitamin A/14.6 mg Vitamin C/323.4 mcg folate/185.9 mg calcium/3.2 mg iron/75.8 mg magnesium/754.8 mg potassium/512.6 mg sodium/0.3 mg thiamin.

MIXED GREENS, TOMATOES, BEANS & CUCUMBER

INGREDIENTS: (4SERVINGS)

Basil leaves (fresh) – ½ cup (well packed)

Extra virgin olive oil – ¼ cup

Red wine vinegar – 3 tbsp

Shallot (properly chopped) – 1 tbsp

Mustard – 2 tsp

Honey – 1 tsp

Salt – ¼ tsp

Pepper (ground) – ¼ tsp

Mixed greens – 10 cups

Cannellini beans (low in sodium & rinsed) – 1 can (15 oz)

Grape tomatoes (in halves) – 1 cup

Cucumber (cut in halves lengthwise; then sliced) – 1 cup

METHOD OF PREPARATION: (TOTAL TIME TAKEN: 25 MINUTES)

1st Step

Put the basil & the shallot into a small food processor. Add in the oil & the vinegar, as well as the honey & mustard. Finally add in the salt plus the pepper. Process the contents until they become nicely smooth. Transfer the processed mixture into a big bowl

2nd Step

Into the bowl of pureed ingredients, add in the beans. Add in the mixed greens as well; and also the cucumber plus the tomatoes. Toss to make a thorough mix.

Nutrition per Single Serving

246 cal/7.5 g protein/21.5 carbs/7.6 g fiber/4.9 g sugar (1 g added)/15.3 g fat (2 g saturated)/4400.6 IU Vitamin A/29.9 mg Vitamin C/189.6 mcg folate/125.6 mg calcium/3.6 mg iron/90.7 mg magnesium/793.3 mg potassium/270.5 mg sodium/0.6 mg thiamin.

BROCCOLI, BELL PEPPERS & PESTO WITH BROWN RICE

INGREDIENTS: (1 SERVINGS)

Broccoli (florets) – 4 cups

Red bell peppers (in quarters) – 2 (of medium size)

Ready pesto – 4 tbsp

Brown rice (already cooked) – 3 cups

Extra virgin olive oil – 3 tbsp

Garlic powder – ½ tsp

Salt – ¼ tsp

Pepper (ground) – ¼ tsp

Red onion (sliced) – 1 cup

Chickpeas (rinsed) – 1 can (15 oz)

METHOD OF PREPARATION: (TOTAL TIME TAKEN: 5 MINUTES)

1st Step

Pre-heat your oven up to 450°F. Put 2 tbsp of oil in a big bowl. Add in the garlic, salt & pepper and whisk the contents. Add in the broccoli, the bell peppers plus the onion; and toss thoroughly

2nd Step

Transfer the contents to a big baking sheet. Roast for around 20 min; ensuring you stir once halfway through (the vegetables should become tender)

3rd Step

Pour the remainder of the oil (1 tbsp) onto the ready rice. Divide the rice into 4 and put each share into a container that is microwave-safe; one with a lid. Share the chickpeas plus the vegetables among the bowls. Top every one of the bowls with a tbsp of pesto.

4th Step

Re-heat every one of the dishes on high in the microwave for between 1 & 2 min.

Nutrition per Single Serving

484 cal/12.4 g protein/64.4 g carbs/10.1 g fiber/7.8 g sugar/20.5 g fat (3.2 g saturated)/4283 IU Vitamin A/144.4 mg Vitamin C/127.1 mcg folate/103.9 mg calcium/2.6 mg iron/109.4 mg magnesium/635.1 mg potassium/460.3 mg sodium/0.4 mg thiamin.

SHRIMP, BEET & ARUGULA-RICH SALAD

INGREDIENTS: (1 SERVINGS)

Arugula (loosely packed) – 2 cups

Beet (cooked & in wedges) – 1 cup

Shrimp (peeled & cooked) – 4 oz

Watercress (loosely packed) – 1 cup

Zucchini (sliced in ribbons) – ½ cup

Fennel (finely sliced) – ½ cup

Barley (cooked) – ½ cup

Extra virgin olive oil – 2 tbsp

White wine vinegar – 1 tbsp

Mustard – ½ tsp

Shallot – ½ tsp

Pepper (ground) – ¼ tsp

Salt – a pinch

Vinaigrette

Fennel fronds (for garnishing)

METHOD OF PREPARATION: (TOTAL TIME TAKEN: 5 MINUTES)

1st Step

Set on a dinner plate the shrimp & arugula; the watercress & the beets; the zucchini & the fennel, as well as the barley.

2nd Step

Take a tiny bowl and in it pour the oil & the vinegar. Add in the mustard; the shallot, the pepper plus the salt. Whisk the ingredients to mix. Next, drizzle this mixture over the prepared salad. Finally, use the fennel fronds to garnish the dish.

Nutrition per Single Serving

584 cal/35 g protein/47 g carbs/9.3 g fiber/17.9 g sugar/29.8 g fat (4.2 g saturated)/214.3 mg cholesterol/2645.3 IU Vitamin A/43.3 mg Vitamin C/217.7 mcg folate/255.5 mg calcium/4.3 mg iron/147 mg magnesium/1506 mg potassium/653.6 mg sodium/0.2 mg thiamin.

CHICKEN BREAST & PESTO WITH MIXED GREEN SALAD

INGREDIENTS: (4 SERVINGS)

Chicken breast (skinless & boneless; also trimmed) – 1 lb

Pesto – ¼ cup

Mayonnaise (low in fat) – ¼ cup

Red onion (well chopped) – 3 tbsp

Extra virgin olive oil – 2 tbsp

Red wine vinegar – 2 tbsp

Salt – ¼ tsp

Pepper (ground) – ¼ tsp

Salad of mixed greens – 8 cups (or a 5 oz package)

Cherry tomatoes (in halves) – 1 pint

METHOD OF PREPARATION: (TOTAL TIME TAKEN: 30 MINUTES)

1st Step

Put the chicken in a saucepan of medium size. Add water into the saucepan, ensuring the water level rises 1" above the chicken. Place the pan over heat until boiling starts. Minimize the heat and cover the pan to allow simmering for between 10 & 15 min (the pink of the chicken should all disappear; even at the center). Remove the chicken from the pan and place it on a chopping board. Cut the chicken to pieces of bite-size when it becomes sufficiently cool.

2nd Step

Put the pesto into a bowl of medium size. Add in the mayonnaise plus the onion and mix. Next, add in the chopped chicken. Toss the bowl to ensure the chicken is well coated

3rd Step

Pour the oil and the vinegar into a big bowl. Add in the salt plus the pepper and whisk the contents. Next, add in the salad of mixed greens plus the tomatoes. Toss to mix properly.

4th Step

Lay out 4 plates and serve on them an equal amount of this green salad. Take the chicken salad and top every one of the plates with an equal share.

Nutrition per Single Serving

324 cal/27.1 g protein/9.2 g carbs/2.3 g fiber/3.2 g sugar (1 g added sugar)/19.7 g fat (4.1 g saturated)/71.4 g cholesterol/1777.3 IU Vitamin A/17.6 mg Vitamin C/57.4 mcg folate/153 mg calcium/2.1 mg iron/47.5 mg magnesium/542.2 mg potassium/453.9 mg sodium/0.1 mg thiamin.

EDAMAME-QUINOA TOSS WITH SPINACH

INGREDIENTS: (1 SERVINGS)

Quinoa (raw, rinsed & well drained) - ½ cup

Edamame – 1 cup

Spinach (fresh leaves) – 1 cup

Water – 1 cup

Tomatoes (medium & seeded; also chopped) – 2

Red onion (chopped) – ½ cup

Olive oil – 2 tbsp

Lemon peeling (well shredded) – 1 tsp

Lemon juice – 2 tbsp

Feta cheese (with minimal fat & crumbled) – ¼ cup

Basil (fresh) – 2 tbsp

Salt – ¼ tsp

Black pepper (fresh & ground) – ¼ tsp

METHOD OF PREPARATION: (TOTAL TIME TAKEN: 5 MINUTES)

1st Step

Take a saucepan of medium size and into it pour in the water and the quinoa . Place the saucepan over heat until the contents begin to boil. Reduce the heat and cover the pan; then let the contents simmer for around 15 min (the liquid should be absorbed and the quinoa tender). 4 min before the quinoa is ready, add in the edamame.

2nd Step

Take a big bowl and transfer the quinoa-based mixture into it. Add in the tomato, onion and the arugula.

3rd Step

Into a tiny bowl, put in the olive oil, the lemon peelings & the lemon juice.. Add in half of the feta cheese and stir. Also add in the basil, pepper & the salt. Mix properly and then transfer the contents to the quinoa-based mixture. Toss to contents for thorough coating

4th Step

Take the remainder of the cheese and sprinkle it on the dish. Serve the meal at room temperature.

Nutrition per Single Serving

237 cal/10.6 g protein/23.3 g carbs/4.8 g fiber/4 g sugar/11.8 g fat (2.1 g saturated)/2.5 mg cholesterol/856 IU Vitamin A/21.4 mg Vitamin C/57.9 mcg folate/108.3 mg calcium/2.3 mg iron/54.6 mg magnesium/320.9 mg potassium/275.9 mg sodium.

GOAT CHEESE, FIG & GREENS SALAD

INGREDIENTS: (1 SERVINGS)

Mixed green vegetables – 2 cups

Figs (dried, stemmed; then sliced) – 4

Goat cheese (fresh & crumbled) – 1 oz

Almonds (slivered & toasted) – 1½ tbsp

Extra virgin olive oil – 2 tsp

Balsamic vinegar – 2 tsp

Honey – ½ tsp

Salt – a pinch

Pepper (ground) – just enough to taste

METHOD OF PREPARATION: (TOTAL TIME TAKEN: 10 MINUTES)

1st Step

Put the greens, the figs & the almonds in a bowl of medium size. Add in the goat cheese and mix the ingredients. Add in the oil and the honey, as well as the vinegar, pepper and the salt. Stir contents for proper mixing.

2nd Step

Top the salad with the ready dressing and then toss for thorough mixing and coating; then serve.

Nutrition per Single Serving

340 cal/10.4 g protein/31.8 g carbs/7 g fiber/21.8 g sugar (3 g added sugar)/21 g fat (5.9 g saturated)/13 mg cholesterol/3288.9 IU Vitamin A/18.1 mg Vitamin C/138.1 mcg folate/186.1 mg calcium/3.2 mg iron/83 mg magnesium/676.2 mg potassium/309.5 mg sodium/0.2 mg thiamin.

WHITE BEAN & VEGGIE RICH AVOCADO SALAD

INGREDIENTS: (1 SERVINGS)

Green vegetable salad (mixed greens) – 2 cups

Cucumber (neatly chopped) – ¾ cup

White beans (rinsed & drained) – 1/3 cup (from a can)

Avocado (neatly diced) – ½

Red wine vinegar – 1 tbsp

Extra virgin olive oil – 2 tsp

Kosher salt – ¼ tsp

Pepper (fresh & ground) – just enough to taste

METHOD OF PREPARATION: (TOTAL TIME TAKEN: 10 MINUTES)

1st Step

Put all the solid ingredients, apart from the seasoning ingredients, in a bowl of medium size and mix until well combined. Add in the salt & the pepper and mix the contents properly to season evenly. Serve the ready salad on a big plate.

Nutrition per Single Serving

360 cal/10.1 g protein/29.7 g carbs/13.3 g fiber/2.9 g sugar/24.6 g fat (3.6 g saturated)/3221 IU Vitamin A/30 mg Vitamin C/261.9 mcg folate/140.1 mg calcium/4.5 mg iron/104 mg magnesium/1291.6 mg potassium/321.3 mg sodium/0.2 mg thiamin.

GREEK-INSPIRED CHICKEN SALAD

INGREDIENTS: (4 SERVINGS)

Chicken (shredded) – 2 cups

Greek vinaigrette (low in calories) – ½ cup

Lemon zest (well shredded) – 1 tsp

Oregano (dried & crushed) – ½ tsp

Romaine lettuce (roughly torn) – 6 cups

Cucumber (medium size; chopped) – 1½ cups

Grape tomatoes (in halves) – 1 cup

Yellow sweet pepper (medium; chopped) – ¾ cup

Red onion (finely sliced & rings put each apart) – ½ cup

Feta cheese (low in fat & crumbled) – ½ cup

Kalamata olives (pitted & in halves) – ¼ cup

Lemon wedges (to use as garnish) – 4

METHOD OF PREPARATION: (TOTAL TIME TAKEN: 20 MINUTES)

1st Step

Put the chicken in a bowl of medium size. Add in half of the vinaigrette. Add in the lemon zest plus the oregano. Mix ingredients; then set the bowl aside.

2nd Step

Take a big salad bowl and throw in the lettuce. Add in the remaining half of the vinaigrette. Put 1½ cups of lettuce into every one of 4 bowls (shallow ones). For each of these smaller bowls, add 1/3 cup of cucumber as topping . Onto the cucumber topping, add ¼ cup of tomatoes, 2 tbsp onion & 3 tbsp sweet pepper. In the middle of each bowl, add in a proportionate amount of the chicken mixture . Sprinkle each dish with 2 tbsp of feta cheese & 1 tbsp of olives.. Serve a lemon wedge alongside every one of the 4 bowls.

Nutrition per Single Serving

220 cal/24.9 g protein/13.3 g carbs/4.1 g fiber/5.2 g sugar/8.2 g fat (2.6 g saturated)/85.3 mg cholesterol/6820.9 IU Vitamin A/87 mg Vitamin C/125.6 mcg folate/111.3 mg calcium/2.2 mg iron/44.3 mg magnesium/620.6 mg potassium/480.6 mg sodium.

SALAD GREENS, QUINOA WITH HUMMUS DRESSING

INGREDIENTS: (4 SERVINGS)

Hummus (original) – 2 tbsp

Quinoa – ½ cup

Salad greens (different types) – 2 cups

Lemon juice – 1 tbsp

Red pepper (chopped & roasted) – 1 tbsp

Chickpeas (well rinsed) – ½ cup

Sunflower seeds (not salted) – 1 tbsp

Parsley (fresh & chopped) – 1 tbsp

Salt – a pinch

Pepper (ground) – a pinch.

METHOD OF PREPARATION: (TOTAL TIME TAKEN: 10 MINUTES)

1st Step

Put the hummus and the lemon juice into a tiny dish. Add in the red peppers and stir. Add in some water as appropriate to give the dressing consistency.

2nd Step

Put the quinoa, chickpeas & the mixed greens into a big bowl. Take the sunflower seeds and use it as topping alongside the parsley. Sprinkle a pinch of salt and pepper as desired. Serve this dish with the hummus dressing.

Nutrition per Single Serving

379 cal/16 g protein/58.5 g carbs/13.2 g fiber/2.9 g sugar/10.5 g fat (1.3 g saturated)/4185.4 IU Vitamin A/45.3 mg Vitamin C/300.1 mcg folate/138.7 mg calcium/5.8 mg iron/155.9 mg magnesium/891.7 mg potassium/606.8 mg sodium/0.3 mg thiamin.

SHRIMP, AVOCADO WITH WHOLE-WHEAT TORTILLA

INGREDIENTS: (4 SERVINGS)

Shrimp (chopped & cooked) – 3 oz

Avocado (diced) – ¼ cup

Tortilla (whole wheat) – 1

Feta cheese (crumbled) – 2 tbsp

Tomato (diced) – ¼ cup

Scallion (well sliced) – 1

Lime juice – 1 tbsp

METHOD OF PREPARATION: (TOTAL TIME TAKEN: 5 MINUTES)

1st Step

Put the shrimp and the feta cheese in a tiny bowl. Add in the avocado & the tomato, as well as the scallion & lime juice. Serve alongside the tortilla.

Nutrition per Single Serving

371 cal/28.8 g protein/34.3 carbs/6.4 g fiber/5.9 sugar/13.7 g fat (4.4 g saturated)/177.4 mg cholesterol/684.5 IU Vitamin A/18.5 mg Vitamin C/6.4 mcg folate/275.4 mg calcium/2.6 mg iron/60.5 mg magnesium/641.4 mg potassium/614.8 mg sodium.

FALAFEL & TAHINI SAUCE WITH FETA CHEESE

INGREDIENTS: (4 SERVINGS)

Falafel (ready & frozen) –1 package (8 oz)

Tahini sauce – ½ cup

Feta cheese (crumbled) – ¼ cup

Water – 2/3 cup

Couscous (whole wheat) – ½ cup

Green beans (fresh) – 1 bag (16 oz)

Kalamata olives (pitted) – ¼ cup

METHOD OF PREPARATION: (TOTAL TIME TAKEN: 20 MINUTES)

1st Step

Read the package and prepare the falafel as per instructions. Set the ready falafel aside to enable cooling.

2nd Step

Boil water in a tiny saucepan. Add in the couscous and cover the pan. Take the pan off the heat and leave it still for around 5 min (the liquid is absorbed in the meantime). Use a fork to fluff the contents; then set the pan aside.

3rd Step

Prepare the fresh green beans as per the instructions on the package

4th Step

Prepare the Tahini sauce and share it among four small containers (these containers should have lids to cover the sauce). Refrigerate the sauce in the containers.

5th Step

Take the ready green beans and share them equally among another 4 small containers (the containers should have lids). Share the couscous, the falafel, the olives and the feta cheese among the 4 containers as topping

6th Step

Use a microwave to re-heat the meal for around 2 min. Apply the Tahini sauce as dressing; then serve the meal.

Nutrition per Single Serving

500 cal/14.8 g protein/54.5 g carbs/11.1 g fiber/7.6 g sugar/27 g fat (4.8 g saturated)/8.3 mg cholesterol/1163.6 IU Vitamin A/23.5 mg Vitamin C/53 mcg folate/147.5 mg calcium/3 mg iron/42 mg magnesium/308 mg potassium/695.5 mg sodium/0.3 mg

CHAPTER 6:

30 MEDITERRANEAN DINNER RECIPES

ROASTED PORTOBELLO MUSHROOM PIZZA

This dinner recipe is complete when accompanied with some arugula salad. These mushrooms as prepared are used in place of the ordinary pizza crust.

INGREDIENTS: (4 SERVINGS)

Portobello mushroom caps – 8 pc each 4oz (gills eliminated)

Olive oil – 2 tbsp

Ground pepper – ½ teaspoon

Tomato sauce – ½ cup

Baby spinach – 2 cups (chopped and packed loosely)

Dried tomatoes (sun-dried) – ½ cup (chopped)

Artichoke hearts – 1 can/14oz (chopped)

Partially skimmed mozzarella cheese – ½ cup (shredded)

Feta cheese – ¼ cup (crumbled)

Italian seasoning – ½ tsp (dried)

Lemon juice – 1 tbsp

Baby arugula – 2 cups (loosely packed)

Basil leaves (fresh) – ¼ cup (in thin slices)

METHOD OF PREPARATION: (TOTAL TIME TAKEN: 45 MINUTES)

1st Step

Prepare the oven by pre-heating it to 400°F. Gently scrape off the gills from the under part of the Portobello caps and discard them. Lay some foil on a big baking sheet; then place a wire-rack on top. Take 1 tablespoon of oil and brush with it the portobello caps. Place the oiled Portobello caps on the wire-rack, with their under parts facing up. Put the rack in the oven and leave the Portobello caps to roast for 10min. Flip the portobello caps and leave them to roast, this time for 5min

2nd Step

Take the rack out of the oven and flip the Portobello caps over with care; meaning the undersides are facing up again. Use ¼ tsp of pepper to season the roasted caps. Use 1 tbsp of sauce smear the inside of every cap. Share among the Portobello caps in equal proportions, the spinach, tomatoes, feta, artichokes and mozzarella. . Take the Italian seasoning and sprinkle over the dish. Return the rack to the oven for the portobello caps to bake and check after 10 min. Remove the portobello caps from the oven within 10 min and 15 min, when the cheese has melted and begun to turn brown. You now have the pizza ready.

3rd Step

In the meantime, take a medium-size bowl and in it mix the remaining pepper and olive oil.. Add the lemon juice into that mixture and mix further. Add in the arugula and then toss to ensure it is well coated with the mixture. You now have the arugula salad.

4th Step

Use the basil to garnish the ready Portobello pizzas.. You can now serve the Portobello mushroom pizzas alongside the arugula salad.

Nutrition per Single Serving

Nutrition per Serving: 264 cal/Protein 14g/Carb 25g/Fiber 7g/Sugar 11g/ Fat 13g (4g saturated)/Cholesterol 15mg/Potassium 1,036mg/Sodium 554mg.

NB:

There are two reasons for removing the mushroom gills: It creates space for the stuffing (otherwise the gills are safe to eat). To prevent the gills from discoloring the other ingredients

OLIVES, RAVIOLI & ARTICHOKES

INGREDIENTS: (4 SERVINGS)

Refrigerated/Frozen spinach & ricotta ravioli – 2 packages (per 8 oz)

Tomato (sun dried) filled oil – ½ cup

Additional oil – 2 tbsp

Artichoke hearts (frozen, thawed & quartered) – 1 package (10 oz)

Cannellini beans (unsalted & rinsed) – 1 can (15 oz)

Kalamata olives (sliced) – ¼ cup

Pine nuts (toasted) – 3 tbsp

Fresh basil (chopped) – ¼ cup

METHOD OF PREPARATION: (TOTAL TIME TAKEN: 45 MINUTES)

1st Step

Boil water in a big pot. Prepare the ravioli as per the directions on the package. Drain the ready ravioli. Add into the pot 1 tbsp of oil

2nd Step

Put the balance of oil (1 tbsp) in a big skillet and heat on medium. Add into the skillet the artichokes and the beans, and sauté for between 2 & 3 min.

3rd Step

Take the tomatoes, basil, olives & pine nuts and fold them in the ready ravioli.

Nutrition per Single Serving

454 cal/15g protein/ 60.9 g carbs/13.1 g fiber/1.8 g sugar/19.2 g fat (3.9 g saturated)/ 20 mg cholesterol/1868 IU Vitamin A/ 21 mg Vitamin C/113.8 mcg folate/136.9 mg calcium/2.7 mg iron/53.2 mg magnesium/470 mg potassium/699.9 mg sodium/0.1 mg thiamin.

SLOW-COOKING QUINOA & ARUGULA

INGREDIENTS: (6 SERVINGS)

Vegetable soup (unsalted) – 2¼ cups

Rinsed raw quinoa – 1½ cups

Red onion (sliced) – 1 cup

Garlic (minced) – 2 tsp (approximately 2 cloves)

Unsalted chickpeas (rinsed & drained) – 1 can/15½oz

Olive oil – 2½ tbsp

Kosher salt – ¾ tsp

Lemon juice (fresh) – 2 tsp

Bell peppers (red) – ½ cup (chopped & roasted)

Baby arugula – 4 cups/4oz

Feta cheese – ½ cup/2oz (crumbled)

Kalamata olives – 12 (diced lengthwise into halves)

Oregano (fresh) – 2 tbsp (chopped)

METHOD OF PREPARATION: (TOTAL TIME TAKEN: 3 HOURS 45 MINUTES)

1st Step

Mix the soup, quinoa and chickpeas in a slow cooker around 6 quarts in size. Add in the onions and garlic and mix. Add in 1½ tsp olive oil plus ½ tsp salt and stir. Cover the cooker and let the mixer cook on low heat until no soup is left (takes between 3 and 4 hours)

2nd Step

Switch off the cooker. Use a fork to fluff the mixture. Put together the remaining olive oil (1 tbsp) and ¼ tsp salt. Add the 2 tsp of lemon juice and mix the three ingredients. Add that mixture into the one in the slow cooker. Add the peppers to the cooker and toss it to mix. Fold the arugula gently and then leave it to wilt a bit (around 10 min). Serve the meal. Take the oregano, the olives and the cheese in turns and sprinkle evenly on each serving.

Nutrition per Single Serving

352 cal/12g protein/46g carb/7g fiber/5g sugar/13g fat (3g saturated)/575mg sodium

NB:

You can serve this dish with grilled chicken if you think some people might want meat as an option.

CRUSTED SALMON WITH WALNUT & ROSEMARY

INGREDIENTS: (4 SERVINGS)

Dijon mustard – 2 tsp

Garlic (minced) – 1 clove

Lemon zest – ¼ tsp

Lemon juice – 1 tsp

Rosemary (fresh & chopped) – 1 tsp

Honey – ½ tsp

Kosher salt – ½ tsp

Red pepper (crushed) – ¼ tsp

Bread crumbs (Panko) – 3 tbsp

Walnuts (thinly chopped) – 3 tbsp

Extra virgin olive oil – 1 tsp

Salmon (skinless fillet) – 1 lb

Cooking spray (from Olive oil)

Parsley (chopped) – for garnishing

Lemon (in wedges) – for garnishing

Some quinoa (or roasted potatoes – as side dish

METHOD OF PREPARATION: (TOTAL TIME TAKEN: 20 MINUTES)

1st Step

Pre-heat oven up to 425°F. Spread parchment paper on a large baking sheet (rimmed)

2nd Step

Put in a tiny bowl, the mustard, honey, garlic, rosemary and lemon zest. Add into the same bowl the salt, red pepper and lemon juice and mix. Mix the panko, oil and walnuts in a different tiny bowl

3rd Step

Lay the salmon on the baking sheet. Spread the mixture on the salmon fillet. Sprinkle the panko mixture on the salmon fillet and press. Apply a light coat of the cooking spray on the coated fish.

4th Step

Bake the salmon until a fork can easily flake it (between 8 & 12 min)

5th Step

Sprinkle the parsley on the baked salmon . Serve the lemon wedges alongside the salmon and quinoa (or the potatoes)

Nutrition per Single Serving

222 cal/24g protein/4g carb/1g sugar/12g fat (2g saturated)/62mg cholesterol/256mg sodium
The meal also has omega 3 fatty acids from salmon & walnuts.

SPAGHETTI SQUASH STUFFED WITH CHEESY SPINACH PLUS ARTICHOKE

INGREDIENTS: (4 SERVINGS)

Spaghetti squash (diced lengthwise in half & seeds extracted) – 1 (2½ pounds)

Water (in 2 half portions) – 3 tbsp

Baby spinach – 1 package (5oz)

Artichoke hearts (thawed then chopped) – 1 package (10 oz)

Cream cheese (in soft cubes with minimal fat) – 4 oz

Parmesan cheese (grated) – ½ cup (put in half portions)

Salt – ¼ tsp

Pepper (ground) – ¼ tsp

Red pepper (crushed) & fresh basil (chopped) – for garnishing

METHOD OF PREPARATION: (TOTAL TIME TAKEN: 25 MINUTES)

1st Step

Put squash in a dish fit for the microwave; sliced side facing down. Add in 2 tbsp water. Put the uncovered dish in the microwave at high heat. Remove when squash is tender (after between 10 & 15 min)

2nd Step

Mix the spinach & the 1 tbsp remainder water in a big skillet. Put mixture on medium heat to cook and keep stirring until spinach has wilted (between 3 & 5 min). Drain spinach and pour it into a big bowl.

3rd Step

Preheat a broiler and put rack within the upmost 1/3rd of the oven

4th Step

Scrape squash off the shells and into your bowl. Put the shells on some baking sheet. Add the artichoke hearts and cream cheese into the bowl with squash . Add also the salt, pepper & parmesan (¼ cup) and stir the mixture. Share the squash mixture among the shells. Top the squash mixture in the shells with the remaining parmesan (¼ cup). Broil the squash mixture for around 3 min (cheese should be golden brown). Take the red pepper & basil and sprinkle on the broiled mixture.

Nutrition per Single Serving

223 cal/10.2g protein/23.3g carb/8.6g fiber/7.1g sugar/10.9g fat (5.7g saturated)/28.2mg cholesterol/IUs 3155 Vitamin A/14.7mg Vitamin C/135.6mcg folate/281.4mg calcium/1.9mg iron/81.9mg magnesium/481.5mg potassium/528.3mg sodium.

NB:

This meal is considered a low-carb substitute for the chicken parmesan served with pasta, which is traditionally popular.

CHICKEN BREASTS STUFFED WITH FETA CHEESE

INGREDIENTS: (8 SERVINGS)

Feta cheese (crumbled) – ½ cup

Bell peppers (red) – ½ cup (chopped & roasted)

Spinach (chopped) – ½ cup

Kalamata Olives (pitted then quartered) – ¼ cup

Fresh basil (chopped) – 1 tbsp

Parsley (flat leaf) – 1 tbsp (chopped)

Garlic – 2 cloves (minced)

Chicken breasts (skinless & boneless) – 4pcs (each 8oz)

Salt – ¼ tsp

Pepper (ground) – ½ tsp

Extra virgin olive oil – 1 tbsp

Lemon juice – 1 tbsp

METHOD OF PREPARATION: (TOTAL TIME TAKEN: 60 MINUTES)

1st Step

Pre-heat oven to reach 400°F. . Mix the feta, spinach, roasted peppers, garlic, basil & parsley; and the olives all in a bowl of medium size

2nd Step

Cut every chicken breast horizontally at its thickest part, in a manner to create a pocket. Use the feta mixture to stuff the pockets of the chicken breasts, 1/3 cup each. Secure each breast pocket with some wooden tooth picks. Sprinkle the salt & pepper evenly all over the chicken

3rd Step

Put the oil in a big skillet and set the heat at medium high. Place the breasts in the pan with their tops facing down. Cook the breasts for around 2 min (until they turn golden). Flip the chicken breasts with care and transfer them to the pan and into the oven. Bake the chicken until the thermometer you use to check the chicken breast's thickest part reads 165°F (between 20 & 25 min). Apply the lemon juice over the chicken in drizzles. Get rid of the wooden tooth picks and proceed to serve the chicken.

Nutrition per Single Serving

179 cal/24.4 g protein/1.9 g carb/0.1 g fiber/1.1 g sugar/7.4 g fat (2.5g saturated)/71 mg cholesterol/1123.7 IU Vitamin A/14.2 mg Vitamin C/10.9 mcg folate/63.3 mg calcium/ 1 mg iron/25.4 mg magnesium/213.5 mg potassium/352 mg sodium/0.1 mg thiamin.

NB:

The purpose of cooking the chicken breasts in the skillet first is to ensure they attain the appealing golden brown color. Meanwhile, the oven baking ensures the cooking is even all through.

PESTO, SHRIMP & QUINOA

INGREDIENTS: (4 SERVINGS)

Pesto (cooked) – 1/3 cup

Balsamic vinegar – 2 tbsp

Extra virgin olive oil – 1 tbsp

Salt – ½ tsp

Ground pepper – ¼ tsp

Shrimp (deveined) – 1 pound

Arugula – 4 cups

Quinoa (cooked) – 2 cups

Cherry tomatoes – 1 cup (divided into halves)

Avocado (diced) – 1

METHOD OF PREPARATION: (TOTAL TIME TAKEN: 25 MINUTES)

1st Step

Whisk the pesto, pepper, salt and vinegar in a big bowl. Add the oil and whisk the mixture. Scoop 4 tbsp of that mixture and pour it into a tiny bowl

2nd Step

Take a skillet of cast iron and place it over medium heat . Add in the shrimp to cook . Keep stirring shrimp for between 4 & 5 min (to be slightly charred). Remove shrimp and place on a plate.

3rd Step

Add into the big bowl the arugula and the quinoa; then toss to ensure proper coating. Share the mixture into 4 separate bowls. Top the mixture with the tomatoes, the avocado & the shrimp. Take the mixture with pesto and share it among the 4 bowls by drizzling around 1 tbsp on each.

Nutrition per Single Serving

429 cal/30.9 g protein/29.3 g carb/7.2 g fiber/5 g sugar/22g fat (3.6 g saturated)/187.5 mg cholesterol/1125.6 IU Vitamin A/ 14.4 mg Vitamin C/108.9 mcg/205.4 mg calcium/2.9 mg iron/130.5 mg magnesium/901.1 mg potassium/571.4 mg sodium/0.2 mg thiamin.

NB:

You can use chicken or steak in place of shrimp if you wish, and you can also add your preferred vegetables.

SALMON, BROCCOLI & SWEET POTATOES

INGREDIENTS: (4 SERVINGS)

Mayonnaise (low fat) – 3 tbsp

Chili powder – 1 tsp

Medium-size sweet potatoes (peeled & diced into cubes) – 2

Olive oil – 4 tsp

Salt – ½ tsp

Ground pepper – ¼ tsp

Broccoli (in florets) – 4 cups (approx.1 medium-size crown)

Salmon (as fillet) – 1¼ lbs (divided into 4 equal portions)

Lime – 1 divided into wedges

Lime –1 (for zesting & juicing)

Feta (crumbled) – ¼ cup

Fresh cilantro (chopped) – ½ cup

METHOD OF PREPARATION: (TOTAL TIME TAKEN: 45 MINUTES)

1st Step

Pre-heat the oven up to 425°F. Lay some foil on a big baking sheet . Use some cooking spray on the foil-covered sheet

2nd Step

Put the mayonnaise & the chili in some tiny bowl.

3rd Step

Into a bowl of medium size, put the sweet potatoes, ¼ tsp of salt, 1/8 tsp of pepper, and 2 tsp of oil.

4th Step

Spread the sweet potato mixture onto the foil-covered baking sheet. Leave the mixture to roast in the oven for 15 min.

5th Step

In the same big bowl, toss in the broccoli, 2 tsp of oil, ¼ tsp of salt & 1/8 tsp of pepper.

6th Step

Take the baking sheet out of the oven. After stirring the sweet potatoes, push them against the pan edges. Place the salmon at the pan's center. Spread your broccoli on the sides of the pan where the sweet potatoes are.

7th Step

Scoop 2 tbsp of your mayonnaise mixture and spread it over the fish.

8th Step

Return the baking sheet into the oven for the sweet potatoes to bake to tenderness; meanwhile the fish will easily flake when poked using a fork (around 15 min).

9th Step

To the remainder of the mayonnaise, add the lime zest and juice; then mix properly.

10th Step

Share the fish among the 4 plates. Top the servings with the cheese and the cilantro.

11th Step

Share the sweet potato dish equally among the 4 plates too. Add to the food the sauce of lime and mayonnaise (drizzle the sauce over). Serve the meal alongside the lime wedges.

Nutrition per Single Serving

504 cal/34 g protein/34 g carbs/7 g fiber/7 g sugar/26 g fat (6 g saturated)/83 mg cholesterol/1211 mg potassium/642 mg sodium

SLOW-COOKED MEDITERRANEAN STEW

INGREDIENTS: (6 SERVINGS)

Tomatoes (fire roasted, diced & unsalted) – 2 cans (per 14 oz)

Vegetable broth (low in sodium) – 3 cups

Onion (chopped) – 1 cup

Carrot (chopped) – ¾ cup

Minced garlic – 4 cloves

Oregano (dried) – 1 tsp

Salt – ¾ tsp

Red pepper (crushed) – ½ tsp

Ground pepper – ¼ tsp

Chickpeas (unsalted) – 1 can (15 oz)

Lacinato kale (stemmed then chopped) – 8 cups (approx. 1 bunch)

Lemon juice – 1 tbsp

Extra virgin olive oil – 3 tbsp

Basil (fresh leaves); split if big in size

Lemon – 6 wedges (not mandatory)

METHOD OF PREPARATION: (TOTAL TIME TAKEN: 6 HOURS 45 MINUTES)

1st Step

In a slow cooker (around 4 quarts in volume), put the onion, tomato and garlic; then add oregano, carrot and the peppers and mix them . Add the vegetable broth into the mixture and cover the cooker. Cook the mixture on low heat for 6hr.

2nd Step

From the cooked mixture, scoop ¼ of the liquid and pour it into a tiny bowl. To the tiny bowl add 2 tbsp chickpeas. Use a fork to mash the chickpeas until they are smooth

3rd Step

Add the remainder of the chickpeas to the slow cooker. Add in the mashed chickpeas too, and also the kale and the lemon juice. Combined these ingredients by stirring. Cover the mixture and let it cook for around 30 min (on low heat); until kale becomes tender

4th Step

Distribute the stew evenly in 6 different bowls. Drizzle the stew with the olive oil. Garnish the dishes with basil. Serve the meal alongside the lemon wedges (if you wish).

Nutrition per Single Serving

191 cal/5.7 g protein/22.9 g carb/5.6 g fiber/6.5 g sugar/7.8 g fat (1 g saturated)/5379 IU Vitamin A/32.7 mg Vitamin C/39.3 mcg folate/128 mg calcium/2.1 mg iron/33.8 mg magnesium/309.5 mg potassium/415.5 mg sodium/0.1 mg thiamin.

GRILLED CHICKEN, GREEK CAULIFLOWER & RICE

INGREDIENTS: (4 SERVINGS)

Extra virgin oil – 6 tbsp

Additional Extra virgin oil – 1 tsp

Cauliflower rice – 4 cups

Red onion (chopped) – 1/3 cup

Salt – ¾

Dill (fresh & chopped) – ½ cup

Chicken breasts (boneless & skinless) – 1 pound

Ground pepper – ½ tsp

Lemon juice – 3 tbsp

Oregano (dried) – 1 tsp

Cherry tomatoes – 1 cup (divided in halves)

Cucumber (chopped) – 1 cup

Kalamata olives (chopped) – 2 tbsp

Feta cheese (crumbled) – 2 tbsp

Lemon wedges – 4

METHOD OF PREPARATION: (TOTAL TIME TAKEN: 30 MINUTES)

1st Step

Pre-heat the grill up to medium. Take 2 tbsp oil and heat it in a big skillet using medium heat. Add into the skillet the onion and the cauliflower, and ¼ tsp salt. Stir the meal as it cooks. The cauliflower should have softened after around 5 min.. Remove the skillet from the heat . Add into the skillet ¼ cup of dill and stir.

2nd Step

Take 1 tsp oil and rub it on the chicken. Sprinkle the chicken with ¼ tsp salt. Sprinkle the chicken with ¼ tsp pepper. Grill the chicken for around 15 min. In between, turn the chicken once. To confirm the chicken is ready, insert a thermometer at the chicken's thickest portion; and if it is ready the reading should have reached 165°F. Cut the chicken breast across.

3rd Step

In a tiny bowl, whisk the remainder of the oil (4 tbsp), the remainder of the salt (¼ tsp), the remainder of the pepper (¼ tsp), together with the lemon juice and the oregano.

4th Step

Take the dish of cauliflower and share it evenly among 4 bowls. Top the bowl dishes with the chicken, feta, cucumber and the tomatoes, and also add the olives. Sprinkle over the remainder of the dill (¼ cup). Take the vinaigrette and drizzle it over the dishes. Serve the lemon wedges alongside the dishes if you so wish.

Nutrition per Single Serving

411 cal/29g protein/9.5g carb/3.1g fiber/4.5 g sugar/27.5 g fat (4.5g saturated)/86.9 mg cholesterol/488 IU Vitamin A/54.3 mg Vitamin C/26.5 mcg folate/68.9 mg calcium/1.2 mg iron/44.5 mg magnesium/560.4 mg potassium/629.8 mg sodium/0.2 mg thiamin.

ARUGULA, PROSCIUTTO PIZZA & CORN

INGREDIENTS: (4 SERVINGS)

Whole wheat (or other pizza dough) – 1 pound

Extra virgin olive oil – 2 tbsp

Garlic (minced) – 1 clove

Mozzarella cheese (part skimmed & shredded) – 1 cup

Kernels of corn – 1 cup

Prosciutto (finely sliced) – 1 oz

Arugula –1½ cups

Fresh basil (roughly torn) – ½ cup

Pepper (ground) – ¼ tsp

METHOD OF PREPARATION: (TOTAL TIME TAKEN: 20 MINUTES)

1st Step

Pre-heat grill up to medium

2nd Step

Sprinkle some flour on a surface and roll out the dough into ovals of 12" length. Sprinkle some four on a baking sheet and place the dough on it. Take 1 tbsp oil & the garlic and mix them in a tiny bowl. Take the dough, cheese, prosciutto & garlic oil and put into the pre-heated grill.

3rd Step

Place the crust onto the grill after oiling the rack (of the grill). Continue grilling the dough until it puffs and becomes slightly brown (between 1 & 2 min). Flip over the crust, then spread all garlic oil over it. Top the crust with the prosciutto, corn & cheese. Grill the crust for a further 2 or 3 min; until all cheese has melted & the crust is a light brown at its bottom. Take the pizza & return it onto your baking sheet.

4th Step

Take the arugula, pepper & basil and use as pizza toppings. Take 1 tbsp oil & drizzle it on the pizza.

Nutrition per Single Serving

436 cal/18.3 g protein/53.1 g carb/3g fiber/5 g sugar/19.9 g fat (4.6 g saturated)/23.6 mg cholesterol/760.4 IU Vitamin A/4.8 mg Vitamin C/33.8 mcg folate/221 mg calcium/0.6 mg iron/ 28.4 mg magnesium/199.2 mg potassium/684.2 mg sodium/1 g sugar (added).

NB

Avoid using cooking spray on a heated grill. Instead, use some paper towel to spread vegetable oil on the heated grill rack.

VEGAN LENTIL SOUP

INGREDIENTS: (1 SERVINGS)

Extra virgin olive oil – 2 tbsp

Yellow onions (chopped) – 1½ cups

Carrots (chopped) – 1 cup

Garlic (minced) – 3 cloves

Tomato paste (unsalted) – 2 tbsp

Vegetable broth (minimal sodium) – 4 cups

Water – 1 cup

Rinsed cannellini beans (unsalted) – 1 can (15 oz)

Dry lentils (mixture of black, brown & green) – 1 cup

Chopped tomatoes (sundried/put in oil then drained) – ½ cup

Salt – ¾ tsp

Pepper (ground) – ½ tsp

Fresh dill (chopped) –1 tbsp (or more)

Red wine vinegar – 1½ tsp

METHOD OF PREPARATION: (TOTAL TIME TAKEN: 5 MINUTES)

1st Step

Heat the oil on medium in a big heavy cooking pot . Add in the onions and the carrots. Stir as the contents cook, for between 3 & 4 min (contents should be tender). Add in the garlic and continue stirring for 1 min (fragrance released). The cauliflower should have Add in the tomato paste and stir constantly for another 1 min (mixture should now be evenly covered or coated).

2nd Step

Add into the cooking pot the cannellini beans and lentils, tomatoes, pepper & salt and stir. Add in the broth and the water and stir further. Leave the contents on medium heat and wait until it boils. Reduce the heat so that the contents begin to simmer. Cover the pot and let the simmering to continue for between 30 & 40 min (the lentils should be tender).

3rd Step

Remove the pot from the heat. Add in the dill & the vinegar and stir. Garnish the contents with 1 tbsp dill. Garnish the contents with the extra dill if you so wish. Serve your meal..

Nutrition per Single Serving

272 cal/7 g fat (1 g saturated)/487 mg sodium/42 g carb/9 g fiber/13 g protein/2 mg niacin-like nutrients/4618 IU Vitamin A.

EGGPLANT-BASED PARMESAN

INGREDIENTS: (6 SERVINGS)

Cooking spray (of olive oil or even canola)

Eggs – 2 big

Water – 2 tbsp

Breadcrumbs (panko) – 1 cup

Parmesan cheese (grated) – ¾ cup

Italian seasoning – 1 tsp

Eggplants – 2 medium size (total of 2 lbs); cut across to slices ¼" in thickness

Salt – ½ tsp

Ground pepper – ½ tsp

Tomato sauce (unsalted) – 1 jar (24 oz)

Basil (fresh leaves) –¼ cup (or more)

Garlic (grated) – ¼ cup

Red pepper (crushed) – ½ tsp

Mozzarella cheese (partly skimmed/also shredded) – 1 cup

METHOD OF PREPARATION: (TOTAL TIME TAKEN: 45 MINUTES)

1st Step

Put racks within the 3rd lowest part of the oven, and within the middle. Pre-heat it to 400°F. Spread 2 baking sheets onto a baking dish, 9" x 13". Apply cooking spray on the baking sheets

2nd Step

Whisk the eggs plus the water in some shallow dish. Put the breadcrumbs, ¼ cup of the parmesan, plus the Italian seasoning in a different shallow dish and mix. Into the dish with egg mixture, dip each piece of eggplant to coat and press to ensure adherence.

3rd Step

Onto the ready baking sheets, arrange the slices of eggplant in one layer. Apply cooking spray generously on the either side of the eggplant and begin baking. Flip the eggplant as you bake it and switch the pans halfway from one rack to the other, for around 30 min. (The eggplant should be tender and a light brown). Use the salt and the pepper to season the dish.

4th Step

Put the tomato sauce, pepper, basil and garlic into a medium-size bowl and mix.

5th Step

Spread around ½ cup sauce on the ready baking dish. Place in order half of the slices of eggplant on top of the sauce. Scoop I cup of sauce and pour on the eggplant, covering it all over. Sprinkle ¼ cup parmesan on the sauce-covered eggplant. Similarly, sprinkle ½ cup of mozzarella. Take the remainder of the sauce & cheese and top the eggplant.

6th Step

Bake the eggplant dish for between 20 & 30 min (sauce should be bubbling & the top golden). Leave it cooling for 5 min. Sprinkle additional basil on the cool dish if you like. Serve the meal.

Nutrition per Single Serving

241 cal/14 g protein/28 g carb/ 6 g fiber/9 g sugar/9 g fat (4 g saturated)/83 mg cholesterol/1227 IU Vitamin A/44.7 mg Vitamin C/84.7 mcg folate/209.4 mg calcium/1.9 mg iron/53.4 mg magnesium/761 mg potassium/553 mg sodium/0.3 mg thiamin.

BBQ SHRIMP, KALE WITH GARLIC & PARMESAN COUSCOUS

INGREDIENTS: (1 SERVINGS)

Chicken broth (low in sodium) – 1 cup

Poultry seasoning – ¼ tsp

Whole wheat couscous – 2/3rd cup

Parmesan cheese (grated) – (1/3rd cup

Butter – 1 tbsp

Extra virgin olive oil – 3 tbsp

Kale (chopped) – 8 cups

Water – ¼ cup

Garlic (crushed) – 1 big clove

Red pepper (crushed) – ¼ tsp

Salt – ¼ tsp

Shrimp (raw, peeled & deveined) – 1 pound

Barbecue sauce – ¼ cup

METHOD OF PREPARATION: (TOTAL TIME TAKEN: 5 MINUTES)

1st Step

Pour the broth into a saucepan of medium size, put in the broth. Add in the poultry seasoning and put over medium heat until it boils. Add in the couscous and stir. Remove saucepan from the heat and cover. Leave the content to rest for 5 min and then use a spoon to fluff it. Add in the parmesan and the butter and stir. Cover the saucepan to keep the content warm.

2nd Step

Put 1 tbsp oil into a big skillet and heat it on medium heat. Add in the kale and stir as you cook it for between 1 & 2 min (kale should be bright green). Add in water and continue cooking with the pan covered, for around 3 min (the kale should now be tender). Reduce the heat and create a well within the kale's central part, and then add in 1 tbsp oil, red pepper & garlic. Leave the content to cook for 15 sec without disturbing it. Stir so that the kale mixes with the rest of the ingredients. Add salt to season . Put the ready content in a covered bowl to keep it warm.

3rd Step

Into the pan, add the 1 tbsp of oil remaining . Add the shrimp into the same pan. Cook the fish as you stir for around 2 min (the fish should now be curled and with a pink color . Remove the pan from the heat, add the barbecue sauce and stir
Serve the fish alongside the kale and the couscous.

Nutrition per Single Serving

414 cal/32.2 g protein/36.4 g carb/5.4 g fiber/7.2 g sugar/16.9 g fat (4.6 g saturated)/195.9 mg cholesterol/3437 IU Vitamin A/38.8 mg Vitamin C/46.2 mcg folate/202.6 mg calcium/2.3 mg iron/60.6 mg magnesium/566.5 mg potassium/606.3 mg sodium

SALMON, FENNEL & TOMATO COUSCOUS

INGREDIENTS: (4 SERVINGS)

Lemon (to zest)– 1

Lemon (As 8 slices) – 1

Salmon (divided into 4 equal portions) – 1¼ pounds

Salt – 1 tsp

Pepper (ground) – ¼ tsp

Tomato pesto – 4 tbsp

Extra virgin olive oil – 2 tbsp

Fennel bulbs (medium size; in wedges ½" thick) – 2 (preserve the fronds)

Israeli couscous (whole wheat preferable) – 1 cup

Scallions (nicely sliced) – 3

Chicken broth (low in sodium) – 1½ cups

Green olives (sliced) – ¼ cup

Pine nuts (toasted) – 2 tbsp

Garlic (sliced) – 2 cloves

METHOD OF PREPARATION: (TOTAL TIME TAKEN: 40 MINUTES)

1st Step

Zest 1 lemon & preserve that zest. Use the salt & pepper to season the salmon. Spread 1½ tsp of pesto on the pieces of salmon

2nd Step

Put 1 tbsp of oil into a big skillet and heat it on medium . Add in ½ the fennel and leave contents to cook for between 2 & 3 min (fennel should turn brown). Transfer contents to some plate. Lower the heat level to medium. Put into the skillet the 1 tbsp oil remaining and the remainder of fennel. Repeat the previous cooking process. Add in the couscous plus the scallions and cook . Stir the contents frequently until the couscous becomes slightly toasted (between 1 & 2 min). Add in the broth, garlic and olives, as well as the pine nuts and stir. Add in the remaining pesto (2 tbsp) & the unused lemon zest.

3rd Step

Take the ready fennel and the salmon and nestle them into the ready couscous. Top the contents with the 8 slices of lemon. Lower the heat to medium and cover contents to cook for between 10 & 14 min (salmon should be well cooked & the couscous tender). Use the fennel fronds for garnishing if/as you wish

Nutrition per Single Serving

543 cal/ 38.3 g protein/46 g carb/7.6 g fiber/6.5 g sugar/24.1 g fat (saturated 3.6 g)/67.3 mg cholesterol/1572.3 IU Vitamin A/23.5 mg Vitamin C/56.3 mcg folate/150.8 mg calcium/2.6 mg iron/76.3 mg magnesium/1160.5 mg potassium/440.7 mg sodium.

CHICKEN, SPINACH, PARMESAN & SKILLET PASTA

INGREDIENTS: (4 SERVINGS)

Penne pasta (gluten-free) – 8 oz

Extra virgin olive oil – 2 tbsp

Chicken breasts/thighs (skinless & boneless) – 1 pound

Salt – ½ tsp

Pepper (ground) – ¼ tsp

Garlic (minced) – 4 cloves

Dry white wine – ½ cup

Lemon (juice & zest) – 1

Spinach (fresh & chopped) – 10 cups

Parmesan cheese (grated) – 4 tbsp

METHOD OF PREPARATION: (TOTAL TIME TAKEN: 60 MINUTES)

1st Step

Cook the pasta as per directions on package. Drain the ready pasta and set it aside.

2nd Step

Pour the oil into a big skillet and heat it on medium. Add in the chicken, pepper & the salt and cook for between 5 & 10 min. Occasionally stir the contents until it is cooked.

3rd Step

Add in the garlic and continue cooking. Stir the contents and cook for around 1 min. Keep stirring as contents cook until the garlic fragrance is released. Add in the wine, the lemon juice plus the zest and stir. Allow the contents to simmer.

4th Step

Remove. . Take the skillet off the heat. Add in the spinach & the ready pasta then stir.

5th Step

Cover the contents and leave still until the spinach wilts.

6th Step

Serve the dish & top every one of the 4 plates with 1 tbsp of parmesan.

Nutrition per Single Serving

335 cal/28.7 protein/24.9 g carb/2 g fiber/1.1 g sugar/12.3 g fat (2.7 g saturated)/66.9 mg cholesterol/ 7100 IU Vitamin A/30.8 mg Vitamin C/154.8 mcg folate/143.6 mg calcium/3.3 mg iron/107.9 mg magnesium/ 684.5 mg potassium/499.2 mg sodium/0.2 mg thiamin.

CHICKEN PEA, QUINOA, CHICK PEA SALAD & VEGETABLES

INGREDIENTS: (2 SERVINGS)

Water – 2/3 cup

Quinoa – 1/3 cup

Coarse salt (like Kosher) – ¼ tsp

Garlic (crushed) – 1 clove

Lemon zest (grated) – 2 tsp

Lemon juice – 3 tbsp

Olive oil – 3 tbsp

Ground pepper – ¼ tsp

Chickpeas (canned & not salted) – 1 cup

Carrot (shredded) – ½ cup

Avocado (diced) – ½

Mixed green vegetables – 1 package (equivalent to 8 cups)

METHOD OF PREPARATION: (TOTAL TIME TAKEN: 25 MINUTES)

1st Step

Boil the water in a tiny saucepan. Add in the quinoa and stir. Lower the heat and let contents simmer for 15 min while the pan is covered . Once the liquid is absorbed, fluff using a fork to have the grains separated. Leave contents for 5 min to cool.

2nd Step

Place the garlic on a chopping board & sprinkle the salt on the garlic. Use one side of some spoon to mash that garlic into paste. Scrape off that garlic paste and put it in a bowl of medium size. Pour in the lemon juice and the zest and whisk. Add in the pepper & the oil and continue to whisk. Take 3 tbsp dressing and put it into a tiny bowl.

3rd Step

Add in the chickpeas, avocado & the carrot. Add in too the dressing from the ordinary bowl . Toss contents gently to make an even mix. Leave contents still for 5 min so that the flavors blend well. Add in the quinoa; then toss to ensure proper coating.

4th Step

Put the vegetables into a big bowl. Add in the dressing of 3 tbsp set aside in a tiny bowl. Serve the vegetables evenly on 2 plates
Top the plates with the mixture of quinoa.

Nutrition per Single Serving

501 cal/12 g protein/47.3 g carb/12.9 g fiber/6.7 g sugar/31.5 g fat (4.3 g saturated)/7120.5 IU Vitamin A/30.2 g Vitamin C/216.1 mcg folate/111.4 mg calcium/3.5 g iron/112.1 mg magnesium/844.2 mg potassium/348 mg sodium.

CHICKEN, GNOCCHI & BRUSSELS SPROUTS

INGREDIENTS: (4 SERVINGS)

Extra virgin olive oil – 4 tbsp

Oregano (fresh & chopped) – 2 tbsp

Garlic (minced) – 2 big cloves

Pepper (ground) – ½ tsp

Salt – ¼ tsp

Brussels sprouts (trimmed & quartered) – 1 pound

Gnocchi (shelf stable) – 1 package (16 oz)

Red onion (sliced) – 1 cup

Chicken thighs (skinless, boneless & trimmed) – 4

Cherry tomatoes (in halves) – 1 cup

Red wine vinegar – 1 tbsp

METHOD OF PREPARATION: (TOTAL TIME TAKEN: 40 MINUTES)

1st Step

Pre-heat the oven up to 450° F

2nd Step

Into a big bowl, pour in 2 tbsp oil, ½ garlic, 1/8 tsp salt, 1 tbsp oregano & ¼ tsp pepper.. Add in the sprouts, onion & the gnocchi; then toss to ensure proper coating. Spread content onto a big baking sheet.

3rd Step

Pour 1 tbsp oil into a big bowl. Add in the balances of oregano, 1 tbsp, pepper, ¼ tsp, salt, 1/8th & the garlic.. Add in the chicken thighs and toss to ensure proper coating. Nestle that chicken into the mixture of vegetables and let content roast for 10 min.

4th Step

Take the bowl off the oven. Add in the tomatoes and stir until contents combine. Roast for a further 10 min to make the sprouts tender & chicken properly cooked. Pour into the mixture the vinegar & the 1 tbsp oil in balance.

Nutrition per Single Serving

604 cal/39.1 g protein/60.6 g carb/6.8 g fiber/4.8 g sugar/23.9 g fat (saturated 4.7 g)/154.3 mg/1224 IU Vitamin A/104.1 mg Vitamin C/89.7 mcg folate/96.8 mg calcium/3.8 mg iron/66 mg magnesium/913.8 mg potassium/657.3 mg sodium/0.3 mg thiamin.

PORTOBELLO MUSHROOMS WITH CAPRESE

INGREDIENTS: (4 SERVINGS)

Extra virgin olive oil – 3 tbsp

Garlic (minced) – 1 clove

Salt – ½ tsp

Pepper (ground) – ½ tsp

Portobello mushrooms (having removed stems & gills) – 4

Cherry tomatoes – 1 cup (divided in halves)

Mozzarella pearls (fresh & drained) – ½ cup

Basil (fresh & finely sliced) – ½ cup

Balsamic vinegar – 2 tsp

METHOD OF PREPARATION: (TOTAL TIME TAKEN: 40 MINUTES)

1st Step

Pre-heat your oven up to 400° F

2nd Step

Take a tiny bowl and pour in 2 tbsp oil, ¼ tsp salt, ¼ tsp pepper & garlic.. Use some silicone brush to coat the mushrooms with the mixture. Place these mushrooms onto some baking sheet. Bake to make the mushrooms for around 10 min to make the mushrooms soft. Take the baking sheet off the heat.

3rd Step

In a bowl of medium size, put the tomatoes, basil & mozzarella. Add in also the ¼ tsp salt remaining, ¼ tsp pepper & 1 tbsp oil. Pour the tomato mixture over the mushrooms. Return baking sheet into the oven for between 12 & 15 min more (The tomatoes should properly wilted & and the cheese well melted). Take ½ tsp vinegar and drizzle on the mushrooms. Now serve.

Nutrition per Single Serving

186 cal/6.3 g protein/6.3 g carb/1.9 g fiber/3.9 g sugar/16 g fat (4.4 g saturated)/5 mg cholesterol/735.3 IU Vitamin A/6.3 mg Vitamin C/37 mcg folate/91.5 mg calcium/0.6 mg iron/19.4 mg magnesium/475 mg potassium/313.3 mg sodium/0.1 mg thiamin.

ROASTED SALMON (SWEET & SPICY) & WILD RICE PILAF

INGREDIENTS: (4 SERVINGS)

Fillets of salmon (skinless) – 5 pcs (1¼ pounds)

Balsamic vinegar – 2 tbsp

Honey – 1 tbsp

Salt – ¼ tsp

Pepper (ground) – 1/8 tsp

Bell pepper (Yellow or red & chopped) – 1 cup

Jalapeno pepper (chopped) – 1

Scallions (green section, finely sliced) – 2

Italian parsley (fresh & chopped) – ¼ cup

Wild rice pilaf – 2 2/3 cups

METHOD OF PREPARATION: (TOTAL TIME TAKEN: 30 MINUTES)

1st Step

Pre-heat the oven up to 425° F. Lay some parchment paper on a baking pan of size 15" by 10. Put the salmon on the pan

Take the vinegar & the honey and whisk them in some tiny bowl. Scoop ½ the mixture and spread it on the salmon. Next, sprinkle the salt & the pepper

2nd Step

Roast your salmon for around 15 min (the salmon should easily flake at its thickest section). Take the remainder of the vinegar and drizzle on the fish.

3rd Step

Take a 10" skillet (non-stick) and coat it using cooking spray. Heat the skillet on medium. Add in the bell pepper plus jalapeno

Cook and stir frequently for between 3 & 5 min . Take skillet off the heat, add in the scallions and stir.

4th Step

Take the mixture of pepper & parsley and use it for topping the salmon fillets. Serve the dish with the pilaf.

Nutrition per Single Serving

339 cal/29.6 g protein/42.5 g carb/3.5 g fiber/6.9 g sugar/5.3 g fat (1.3 g saturated)/53 mg cholesterol/1486.2 IU Vitamin A/47.8 mg Vitamin C/66.2 mcg folate/65.6 mg calcium/2.2 mg iron/94 mg magnesium/775.7 mg potassium/442.2 mg sodium/0.3 mg thiamin/3 g added sugars.

SMOKED MOZZARELLA & ROLLS OF ZUCCHINI LASAGNA

INGREDIENTS: (1 SERVINGS)

Zucchini (trimmed) – 2 (big size)

Extra virgin olive oil – 2 tsp

Pepper (ground) – ½ tsp

Salt – ¼ tsp

Mozzarella cheese (smoked & shredded) – 8 tbsp

Parmesan cheese (grated) – 3 tbsp

Egg (slightly beaten) – 1

Ricotta (partly skimmed) – 1½ cup

Spinach (thawed & dried by squeezing) – 1 package (10 oz)

Garlic (minced) – 1 clove

Marinara sauce (low in sodium) – ¾ cup

Basil (fresh & chopped) – 2 tbsp

METHOD OF PREPARATION: (TOTAL TIME TAKEN: 5 MINUTES)

1st Step

Place racks within the oven's upper third & lower third. Pre-heat the oven up to 425° F. Apply cooking spray onto 2 baking sheets

2nd Step

Cut the zucchini into slices along their lengths to produce 24 slices (every one 1/8" thick). Take a big bowl and put in the zucchini, ¼ tsp pepper & 1/8 tsp salt. Pack the zucchini as single layers on the ready pans

3rd Step

Bake zucchini for around 10 min until it becomes tender; turn once. In a bowl of medium size, put in the egg and ricotta, the spinach and garlic, and the remainder of the mozzarella (6 tbsp) and the parmesan (2 tbsp), ¼ tsp pepper plus 1/8 tsp salt. Take ¼ cup of marinara and spread it on a baking dish, 8" by 8" . Take 1 tbsp ricotta mixture and put it close to the bottom of every zucchini strip. Roll it well and then place it within the baking dish, seam side facing down. Repeat process and make use of the zucchini & filling balance. Use ½ cup of the marinara sauce to top the prepared rolls. Sprinkle the rolls using the balance of cheese mixture.

4th Step

Take the zucchini rolls and bake them for around 20 min (they should be bubbly & with some slight browning on the outside). Set them aside for 5 min and then sprinkle the rolls with the basil. Serve your meal.

Nutrition per Single Serving

315 cal/22.2 g protein/16.8 g carb/3.5 g fiber/7.8 g sugar/18.6 g fat (9.1 g saturated)/96.5 mg cholesterol/5833 IU Vitamin A/32.3 mg Vitamin C/118.4 mcg folate/507 mg calcium/2.3 mg iron/82.8 mg magnesium/843.5 mg potassium/561.1 mg sodium.

MEDITERRANEAN FISH, MUSHROOMS & WILTED GREENS

INGREDIENTS: (4 SERVINGS)

Olive oil – 3 tbsp

Sweet onion (large & sliced) – ½

Cremini mushrooms (sliced) – 3 cups

Garlic (sliced) – 2 cloves

Kale (chopped) – 4 cups

Tomato (diced) – 1

Mix of Mediterranean herbs – 2 tsp

Lemon juice – 1 tbsp

Salt – ½ tsp

Pepper (ground) – ½ tsp

Tilapia fillet (or cod) – 4 pcs

Parsley (fresh & chopped) – for garnishing

METHOD OF PREPARATION: (TOTAL TIME TAKEN: 25 MINUTES)

1st Step

Put 1 tbsp of oil in a big saucepan and heat it on medium. Add in the onion and cook for between 3 & 4 min and occasionally stir (onion should be translucent). Add in the garlic & the mushroom and continue to stir occasionally for between 4 & 6 min (the mushrooms should have released their moisture and begun to become brown). Add in the kale, the tomato, and the herb mixture. Cook for between 5 & 7 min and stir occasionally (kale should have wilted & mushrooms become tender). dd the lemon juice, ¼ tsp pepper & ¼ tsp salt. Take the saucepan off the heat, cover it and maintain its warmth.

2nd Step

Take the fish and sprinkle it on the herb mixture remaining. Sprinkle too ¼ tsp salt & ¼ tsp pepper. Take the balance of oil (2 tbsp) and use a big non-stick skillet to heat it on medium. Add in the fish and then cook it both sides for between 2 & 4 min (the fish should turn opaque). Serve the fish onto 4 plates (or on a platter). Top the fish and surround it with the vegetables Sprinkle the dish with parsley as you wish.

Nutrition per Single Serving

214 cal/18 g protein/11 g carb/3 g fiber/4 g sugar/fat 11 g (2 g saturated)/45 mg cholesterol/736 mg potassium/598 mg sodium

CHICKEN & TOMATO-BALSAMIC SAUCE

INGREDIENTS: (1 SERVINGS)

Chicken breasts (skinless & boneless)– 2 (each 8 oz)

Salt – ½ tsp

Pepper (ground) – ½ tsp

Wheat flour (whole) – ¼ cup

Extra virgin olive oil – 3 tbsp

Cherry tomatoes – ½ cup

Shallot (sliced) – 2 tbsp

Balsamic vinegar – ¼ cup

Chicken broth (low level sodium) – 1 cup

Garlic (minced) – 1 tbsp

Fennel seeds (toasted & mildly crushed) – 1 tbsp

Butter – 1 tbsp

METHOD OF PREPARATION: (TOTAL TIME TAKEN: 5 MINUTES)

1st Step

Slice the chicken breasts horizontally in halves to produce 4 parts. Put the chicken on some chopping board & cover using some plastic wrapping. Pound the chicken using a meat mallet's smooth part (or use a heavy pan) to make the thickness even (around ¼"). Sprinkle ¼ salt & ¼ pepper on the chicken. Pour the flour in a dish that is shallow and then dredge the ready cutlets so that both sides are well coated. Shake off the excess flour.

2nd Step

Pour 2 tbsp oil into a big skillet on medium. Add in 2 chicken pcs & cook each of the sides for between 2 & 3 min (turn the pieces once until the chicken has browned). Serve the ready content to a big plate & then use foil to cover it so that it remains warm. Repeat the process with the remainder of the chicken.

3rd Step

Take the remainder of the oil (1 tbsp) and pour into the pan. Add in the tomatoes & the shallot and cook for between 1 & 2 min. Stir occasionally until the content becomes soft. Add in the remainder of the oil (1 tbsp), the tomatoes and the shallot. Stir occasionally as the contents cook for between 1 & 2 min. Add in the vinegar and allow the contents to boil. Scrape those parts that have browned from the base of the pan as cooking continues; and that should take around 45 sec. The vinegar amount will have dropped by half.. Add in the broth, the garlic and fennel seeds, as well as the remainder of the salt (¼ tsp) and the pepper (¼ tsp). Stir as you cook for between 4 & 7 min, when the sauce should have diminished by around a half. Put the pan off the heat . Put in the butter and stir, pour the sauce all over your chicken and then serve.. You may serve this dish alongside whole wheat spaghetti.

Nutrition per Single Serving

294 cal/25.4 g protein/9.5 g carb/1.5 g fiber/3.4 g sugar/16.7 g fat (4.1 g saturated)/70.3 mg cholesterol/263.3 IU Vitamin A/4 mg Vitamin C/7.7 mcg folate/45.8 mg calcium/2 mg iron/33.9 mg magnesium/363.2 mg potassium/370.6 mg sodium.

BAKED RAVIOLI, MUSHROOM BOLOGNESE PLUS RED PEPPER

INGREDIENTS: (4 SERVINGS)

Whole wheat bread crumbs – 1 cup

Parmesan cheese (well grated) – over ¼ cup

Italian seasoning – ½ cup

Egg – 1

Water – 1 tbsp

Cheese ravioli (fresh) – 1 pound

Extra virgin olive oil – 1 tbsp

Red bell pepper (diced) – 1

Mushroom (chopped) – 2 cups

Walnuts (well chopped) – 1/3 cup

Marinara sauce (low in sodium) – 2 cups

METHOD OF PREPARATION: (TOTAL TIME TAKEN: 35 MINUTES)

1st Step

Pre-heat the oven up to 425° F. Put some wire rack on some baking sheet & apply cooking spray

2nd Step

Take a shallow dish and put in the breadcrumbs, the Parmesan & the Italian seasoning and mix them. Take a different shallow dish and use it to whisk the egg plus the water . Dip the ravioli in the beaten egg and let the excess amount fall off. Coat that ravioli using the mixture of bread crumbs while pressing for adherence. Place the ravioli on the rack and give the ravioli a slight touch of the cooking spray.

3rd Step

Take the ravioli and bake it for around 15 min (it should turn crispy & golden brown)

4th Step

Put oil in a big saucepan and heat on medium. Add in the bell pepper & the mushroom and cook for around 4 min (content should become soft). Add in the walnuts & stir as you cook for a minute. Add in marinara & continue cooking for a further 2 min (content should become well hot)

5th Step

Take the sauce & the extra parmesan and serve it alongside the ravioli.

Nutrition per Single Serving

479 cal/19.6 g protein/48.5 g carb/6.2 g fiber/9.2 g sugar/fat23.2 g (6.2 g saturated)/93 mg cholesterol/2464.7 IU Vitamin A/58 mg Vitamin C/40.4 mcg folate/239.6 mcg calcium/3.4 mg iron/26.6 mg magnesium/266.7 mg potassium/501.1 mg sodium/0.1 mg thiamin.

SEARED HALIBUT, TOMATOES & CORN WITH CREAM

INGREDIENTS: (4 SERVINGS)

Corn (husked) – 4 ears

Whole milk – 1½ cups

Garlic – 3 cloves

Thyme (fresh) – 1 sprig

Tomatoes (chopped) – 3 cups

Basil (fresh & chopped) – 3 tbsp

Extra virgin olive oil – 2 tbsp

Salt – ¾ tsp

Butter – 1 tbsp

Shallot (chopped) – ¼ cup

Flour (all purpose) – 2 tbsp

Parmesan cheese (grated) – 2 tbsp

Pepper (ground) – ½ tsp

Halibut (divided into 4 parts) – 1¼ pounds

METHOD OF PREPARATION: (TOTAL TIME TAKEN: 40 MINUTES)

1st Step

Take the kernels off the cobs and put aside. Break those cobs into halves and put them in a big saucepan. Add in the milk, thyme & 2 cloves of garlic. Cook on medium heat and wait for content to simmer along the edges. Take the saucepan off the heat, cover the content and set them aside for 10 min as it steeps. Strain contents into some tiny bowl and get rid of the remnant solids.

2nd Step

Grate the remainder of garlic (1 clove) over a bowl of medium size. Take the tomatoes and the basil, 1 tbsp oil & ¼ tsp salt and add into the bowl. Stir the contents and then set the bowl aside.

3rd Step

Use a pan to melt the butter on medium heat. Add in the shallots & proceed to cook for around a minute as you stir. Take the preserved corn kernels and proceed to cook them for around 3 min. Ensure to stir occasionally until the corn begins to soften. Sprinkle the pan of corn with the flour and give it 30 sec to cook. Stir the pan as you slowly pour in the milk. Reduce the heat so that the pan remains simmering. Cover pan and continue to cook contents for a further 5 min (the liquid should be thick by now). Add in the Parmesan, ¼ tsp pepper & ¼ tsp salt and keep stirring. Cover the pan and set it aside.

4th Step

Take the remainder of the salt (¼ tsp) and the pepper (¼ tsp) and sprinkle on the halibut. Take the remainder of the oil (1 tbsp) and pour it into a big skillet that is non-stick. Heat the skillet on medium, then add in the halibut, and proceed to cook for between 5 & 7 min (halibut should acquire a slight brown). Turn only once.

5th Step

Take the creamed corn plus tomatoes set aside, and serve them alongside the halibut.

Nutrition per Single Serving

422 cal/35.3 g protein/34.8 g carb/4 g fiber/14.7 g sugar/17.2 g fat (5.7 g saturated)/88.4 mg cholesterol/1906.8 IU Vitamin A/27.6 mg Vitamin C/101.3 mcg folate/165.3 mg calcium/1.6 mg iron/100.9 mg magnesium/1395.7 mg potassium/641.1 mg sodium/0.4 mg thiamin.

GREEK BURGERS & HERB-RICH FETA SAUCE

INGREDIENTS: (4 SERVINGS)

Greek yogurt (fat free & plain) – 1 cup

Feta cheese (crumbled) – ¼ cup

Oregano (fresh & chopped) – 3 tbsp

Lemon zest – ¼ tsp

Lemon juice – 2 tsp

Salt – ¾ tsp

Red onion (small) – 1

Lamb (ground) – 1 pound

Pepper (ground) – ½ tsp

Pitas (whole wheat) – 2 (split in halves & warmed)

Cucumber (sliced) – 1 cup

Plum tomato (well sliced) – 1

METHOD OF PREPARATION: (TOTAL TIME TAKEN: 25 MINUTES)

1st Step

Pre-heat the grill to medium level

2nd Step

Take the yogurt, lemon zest & juice, the feta, ¼ tsp salt and 1 tbsp oregano and pour into a tiny bowl; then mix.

3rd Step

Cut the onion into slices of ¼" thickness (making a ¼ cup). Chop additional onion finely to make another ¼ cup. Preserve any surplus onion . Take the chopped ¼ cup of onion and mix it with the meat in some big bowl. Add in the 2 tbsp oregano remaining . Add in ½ tsp pepper & ½ tsp salt. From the mixture, create 4 patties of oval shape, whose sizes are 4" by 3"

4th Step

Grill your burgers for between 4 & 6 min for each side and ensure to turn them once. The thermometer should ultimately read 160° F.. Serve with the slices of onion, tomato & cucumber, and alongside the sauce.

Nutrition per Single Serving

375 cal/29.8 g protein/23.5 g carb/2.5 g fiber/4.4 g sugar/18.1 g fat (saturated 7.8 g)/85.9 mg cholesterol/262.9 IU Vitamin A/6.7 mg Vitamin C/39.2 mcg folate/153.4 mg calcium/2.6 mg iron/57.6 mg magnesium/510.2 mg potassium/775.2 mg sodium.

ROAST FISH & VEGETABLES

INGREDIENTS: (4 SERVINGS)

Fingerling potatoes (split lengthwise into 2) – 1 pound

Olive oil – 2 tbsp

Garlic (roughly chopped) – 5 cloves

Sea salt – ½ tsp

Black pepper (fresh & ground) – ½ tsp

Salmon fillet (skinless) – 4 pieces (around 6 oz each)

Sweet peppers (any type diced to form rings) – 2 medium-size

Cherry tomatoes – 2 cups

Parsley (fresh & chopped) – 1½ cups

Kalamata olives (pitted & cut into halves) – ¼ cup

Oregano (fresh) – ¼ cup (or 1 tbsp dried)

Lemon (crushed) – 1

METHOD OF PREPARATION: (TOTAL TIME TAKEN: 55 MINUTES)

1st Step

Pre-heat the oven up to 425° F. Put the potatoes into a big bowl . Drizzle on the potatoes 1 tbsp oil & also sprinkle them with the garlic. Add 1/8 tsp salt and 1/8 tsp black pepper. Toss the contents to ensure proper coating. Transfer the contents to some baking pan of size 15" by 10" and use foil to cover it. Roast the contents for 30 min.

2nd Step

Put the salmon, sweet peppers and tomatoes in one bowl. Add in the olives and parsley, the oregano, 1/8 black pepper & 1/8 salt. Drizzle the remainder of oil (1 tbsp) on the contents and toss to ensure proper coating.

3rd Step

Rinse the salmon and pat it dry
Sprinkle it with the remainder of the salt (¼ tsp) & remaining black pepper. Use a spoon to scoop the mixture with sweet pepper and add it onto the potatoes. Top that dish with the salmon. Roast the contents while uncovered for a further 10 min (the salmon should flake)

4th Step

Extract zest out of the lemon and then squeeze the juice onto the salmon with the vegetables. Sprinkle the zest over and serve.

Nutrition per Single Serving

422 cal/32.9 g protein/31.5 g carb/5.7 g fiber/6.6 g sugar/18.6 g fat (2.4 g saturated)/78 mg cholesterol/2990 IU Vitamin A/232.7 mg Vitamin C/130.8 mcg folate/103.5 mg calcium/4 mg iron/102.1 mg magnesium/1740.6 mg potassium/593.1 mg sodium.

EASY PEA WITH SPINACH CARBONARA

INGREDIENTS: (1 SERVINGS)

Extra virgin olive oil – 1½ tbsp

Panko breadcrumbs (whole wheat) – ½ cup

Garlic (minced) – 1 tiny clove

Parmesan cheese (grated) – 8 tbsp

Parsley (fresh & chopped) – 3 tbsp

Egg yolk – from 3 eggs

Whole egg – 1

Pepper (ground) – ½ tsp

Salt – ¼ tsp

Linguine (fresh) – 1 package (9 oz)

Baby spinach – 8 cups

Peas – 1 cup

Water – 10 cups

METHOD OF PREPARATION: (TOTAL TIME TAKEN: 5 MINUTES)

1st Step

Pour the water into a big pot and boil it on high level heat.

2nd Step

Use a big skillet to heat the oil on medium level . Add in the breadcrumbs plus the garlic. Cook the contents and stir frequently for around 2 min (contents should be toasted). Transfer the cooked contents into a tiny bowl. Pour in 2 tbsp of Parmesan & parsley and set the tiny bowl aside.

3rd Step

Take the remainder of the Parmesan (6 tbsp) and put it into a bowl of medium size. Add in the egg yolks plus the whole egg, pepper as well as the salt. Whisk the contents.

4th Step

Boil the pasta for a minute, ensuring to stir occasionally. Add in the spinach and the peas and continue to cook for an additional minute (the pasta should be tender). Preserve ¼ cup cooking water, then drain the pasta and pour it into a big bowl.

5th Step

Mix the preserved cooking water and the mixture of egg and embark on whisking the mixture slowly. Slowly by slowly, add in the pasta mixture as you use tongs to toss it. Top the dish with the mixture of breadcrumbs and serve.

Nutrition per Single Serving

430 cal/20.2 g protein/54.1 g carb/8.2 g fiber/2.5 g sugar/14.5 g fat (3.9 g saturated)/223.4 mg cholesterol/8198 IU Vitamin A/50.5 mg Vitamin C/53 mcg folate/246.1 mg calcium/6.1 mg iron/99.6 mg magnesium/160 mg potassium/586.4 mg sodium.

SALMON, BAGNA CAUDA & VEGETABLES

INGREDIENTS: (4 SERVINGS)

Fingerling potatoes – 1 pound
(Or sweet potatoes split into ½" wedges)

Broccolini (trimmed) – 1 bunch

Extra virgin olive oil – 1 tbsp

Salt – ½ tsp

Salmon – 1 pound

Fennel bulb– 1
(diced into ½" wedges & fronds preserved)

Belgian endive (leaves set apart) – 2 heads

Radicchio (in ½" wedges) – ½ head

For Bagna Cauda

Extra virgin olive oil – 1/3 cup

Garlic (thinly diced) – 2 cloves

Anchovy fillets – 8

Sherry vinegar – 2 tbsp

Butter – 1 tbsp

METHOD OF PREPARATION: (TOTAL TIME TAKEN: 40 MINUTES)

1st Step

Pre-heat the oven up to 425° F. Take a big baking sheet and apply cooking spray on it

2nd Step

Put the potatoes (or sweet potatoes) plus the broccolini into some big bowl. Add in 1 tbsp oil & ¼ tsp salt and mix. Pick out the potatoes and transfer them onto the ready baking sheet (the broccolini remains in your bowl). Roast those potatoes for 15 min and in between ensure to turn them once.

3rd Step

Align the potatoes along the baking sheet edges . Take the salmon and position it around the center. Use ¼ tsp salt to season the salmon. Take the broccolini and align it around the fish. Roast the contents for between 6 & 10 min (to ensure vegetables become soft and the salmon is cooked just enough)

4th Step

(Preparation of the Bagna Cauda). Pour oil in a tiny saucepan and add garlic as you heat on medium level for 2 min (the garlic should begin to release its fragrance). Add in the anchovies & then crush them lightly until you see them flake. Add in the vinegar and the butter and then cook on a very low level of heat. That additional cooking should take 2 min.

5th Step

Take a platter and neatly arrange the salmon and the potatoes. Then add the broccolini alongside the fennel radicchio and the endive. Garnish the dish with the fennel fronds earlier set aside.

Serve the dish with the bagna cauda (which can be used for dipping or even drizzling). You can also serve the dish with some crusty bread & a glass of white wine.

Nutrition per Single Serving

537 cal/31.1 g protein/35.2 g carb/7 g fiber/5.1 g sugar/30.4 g fat (6.3 g saturated)/67.4 mg cholesterol/2095.4 IU Vitamin A/86.2 mg Vitamin C/82.3 mcg folate/153.2 mg calcium/2.3 mg iron/74.4 mg magnesium/1481.5 mg potassium/704.6 mg sodium.

GREEN SHAKSHUKA, FETA, CHARD & SPINACH

INGREDIENTS: (6 SERVINGS)

Extra virgin oil – 1/3 cup

Onion (chopped) – 1 large

Chard (stemmed & chopped) – 12 oz

Spinach (mature, stemmed & chopped) – 12 oz

White wine (dry) – ½ cup

Jalapeno (in fine slices) – 1

Garlic (in fine slices) – 2 cloves

Kosher salt – ¼ tsp

Pepper (ground) – ¼ tsp

Chicken broth (low in sodium) –½ cup

Butter (unsalted) – 2 tbsp

Eggs – 6

Goat cheese (crumbled) – ½ cup

METHOD OF PREPARATION: (TOTAL TIME TAKEN: 30 MINUTES)

1st Step

Put oil in a big skillet and let it heat on medium. Add in your onion and stir as it cooks for 7 or 8 min. (until it becomes soft but before browning). Add in the chard & the spinach (continually in little amounts as you stir). After 5 min the vegetables should have wilted. . Add in the wine, garlic, pepper, jalapeno and salt; and stir occasionally as contents cook. Wait for between 2 & 4 min, when the wine is fully absorbed and the garlic soft. Add in the butter & the broth and stir for between 1 or 2 min. (The butter should be well melted and a little of the liquid absorbed)

2nd Step

Crack eggs and pour content over the hot vegetables. Cover the skillet and continue cooking on medium heat for between 3 & 5 min (the whites should be set by now). Take the skillet off the cooker . Sprinkle the cheese onto the contents and cover the skillet. Wait for 2 min and then serve the meal.

Nutrition per Single Serving

296 cal/10.7 g protein/8.5 g carb/2.7 g fiber/2.9 g sugar/23.4 g fat (7.2 g saturated)/ 204.6 cholesterol/9238.8 IU Vitamin A/37.9 mg Vitamin C/150.2 mcg folate/170.8 mg calcium/3.6 mg iron/103.8 mg magnesium/668.8 mg potassium/417.6 mg sodium.

CHAPTER 7:

8 ADDITIONAL MEDITERRANEAN SALADS

MASSIVE MEDITERRANEAN GREEK SALAD

INGREDIENTS: (6 SERVINGS)

Red wine vinegar – 2 tbsp

Lemon juice (fresh) – 1 tbsp

Oregano (dried) – ½ tsp

Pepper (fresh & ground) – just enough to taste

Kosher salt – a pinch

Extra virgin olive oil – ¼ cup

Cucumber (tiny & chopped) – 1

Cherry tomatoes (in halves) – 1 cup

Lettuce (large & roughly chopped) – 1 head

Kalamata olives – ½ cup

Caperberries (big in size) – ½ cup

Peppadew peppers (chopped) – ½ cup

Red onion (finely sliced) – ½

METHOD OF PREPARATION: (TOTAL TIME TAKEN: 20 MINUTES)

1st Step

Pour the vinegar and the lemon juice into a big bowl. Add in the oregano, ¼ tsp salt & ¼ tsp pepper. Whisk these ingredients to mix them well. Add also the olive oil and whisk the contents to ensure this salad dressing is smooth.

2nd Step

Add your cucumber to the bowl with salad dressing; and also the tomatoes and the caperberries. Also add the lettuce and the olives, as well as the peppadews and the red onion. Toss to ensure all the ingredients are well coated with the dressing. Season your salad with some salt & pepper.

Nutrition per Single Serving

146 cal/8 g carbs/12 g fat (2 g saturated)/358 mg sodium/3 g fiber/zero cholesterol

TRADITIONAL MEDITERRANEAN GREEK RECIPE FOR SALAD

INGREDIENTS: (6 SERVINGS)

Red Onion (medium) – 1

Tomatoes (medium & juicy) – 4

English cucumber (part-peeled to form some pattern)

Green bell pepper (well cored) – 1k

Greek Kalamata olives (pitted) – just a handful

Kosher salt – a pinch

Extra virgin olive oil – 4 tbsp

Red wine vinegar – 2 tbsp

Feta cheese (big pieces)

Oregano (dried) – ½ tbsp

METHOD OF PREPARATION: (TOTAL TIME TAKEN: 15 MINUTES)

1st Step

Split the red onion in halves; then thinly cut each half into pieces resembling half-moon. Slice tomatoes into big pieces. Take the cucumber and cut it into half along the length. Make thin slices from the halved pieces of cucumber (½" thick). Make rings out of your bell pepper.

2nd Step

Put all the ingredients in a big salad dish. Add a big handful of olives to the dish. Use a pinch of the kosher salt and a little oregano to season.

3rd Step

Take the olive oil and pour it on the prepared salad. Take the red wine vinegar and pour it on the same salad. Toss the dish gently to ensure the ingredients are well mixed and coated (Be mild with the mixing). Add the pieces of feta on the salad and sprinkle some more oregano; then serve.

Nutrition per Single Serving

102.9 cal/0.7 g protein/4.7 g carbs/9.5 g fat (1.3 g saturated)/2.8 mg sodium/135 mg potassium/1.1 g fiber/125.9 IU Vitamin A/18.7 mg Vitamin C/20.9 mg calcium/0.5 mg iron.

MEDITERRANEAN GREEK-LIKE SALAD WITH MESCLUN

INGREDIENTS: (6 SERVINGS)

Mix of arugula, oak leaf, chervil & mache (mesclun) – 4 cups

Red pepper (bite-size bits) – 1

Cucumber (peeled; then sliced) – 1

Grape tomatoes – ½ cup

Red onion (finely sliced) – ¼ cup

Kalamata olives (pitted) – ½ cup

Extra virgin olive oil – ½ cup

Lemon juice – ¾ cup

Goat cheese (crumbled) – 4 oz

Salt – a pinch

Pepper – just sufficient to give taste

METHOD OF PREPARATION: (TOTAL TIME TAKEN: 15 MINUTES)

1st Step

Put all the vegetables in a bowl. Add in the olives. Add in the oil & the juice; then toss the contents

2nd Step

Top the salad with the goat cheese; then serve.

Nutrition per Single Serving

245 cal/4 g protein/5 g carbs/24 g fat (6 g saturated)/17 mg cholesterol/3 g sugar/1 g fiber/395 mg sodium/183 mg potassium/1094 IU Vitamin A/35 mg Vitamin C/112 mg calcium/1 mg iron.

TOMATO, CUCUMBER & PARSLEY RICH SALAD

INGREDIENTS: (6 SERVINGS)

Roma tomatoes (sliced) – 3 cups

Cucumber (large) – 1

Parsley (chopped fresh leaves) – ¾ cup

Kosher salt – a pinch

Sumac (ground) – 1 tsp

Extra virgin olive oil – 2 tbsp

Lemon juice (fresh) – 2 tsp

METHOD OF PREPARATION: (TOTAL TIME TAKEN: 10 MINUTES)

Put the tomatoes, parsley & the cucumber in one bowl; then mix them.Season those ingredients with the salt; then toss

Let the salad rest for around 5 min; then add your sumac. Add in too the oil plus the lemon juice. Gently toss the salad; then serve.

Nutrition per Single Serving

62.5 cal/1 g protein/4.8 g carbs/4.9 g fat (0.7 g saturated; 0.6 g polyunsaturated & 3.4 g monounsaturated)/2.6 g sugar/1.2 g fiber/7 mg sodium/252.1 mg potassium/991.2 IU Vitamin A/17.2 mg Vitamin C/22 mg calcium/0.7 mg iron.

FARRO-RICH SALAD WITH CHICKEN

INGREDIENTS: (6 SERVINGS)

Red wine vinegar – 1/3 cup

Mustard – 1½ tbsp

Garlic (small & minced) – 1 clove

Kosher salt – ¾ tsp

Pepper (ground) – ½ tsp

Extra virgin olive oil – ½ cup

Farro – 1 cup

Water – 3 cups

Chicken (skinless & boneless; also trimmed) – 1½ lb

Kosher salt – ½ tsp

Pepper (ground) – ¼ tsp

Fennel bulb (nicely cored & also chopped)

Carrot (nicely diced) – 1 cup

English cucumber (seeded & chopped) – 1 cup

Red onion (well chopped) – ½ cup

Parsley (chopped) – ¼ cup

Basil (fresh & sliced) – ¼ cup

Mint (fresh & well sliced) – ¼ cup

Arugula (chopped after eliminated hard stems) – 2 cups

Black olives (cured with oil; and sliced) – ¼ cup

METHOD OF PREPARATION: (TOTAL TIME TAKEN: 60 MINUTES)

1st Step

Prepare the salad dressing by whisking the vinegar, the garlic & the mustard in a bowl of medium size. Add in ¾ salt & ½ tsp pepper and continue whisking.

2nd Step

Prepare the salad by first of all putting the water in some medium-size saucepan and boiling it. Add in the farro as you minimize the heat. Cover the saucepan and let the contents simmer for between 15 & 25 min (the farro should become tender). Drain the contents and put the farro into a big bowl.

3rd Step

Toss 1/3 cup salad dressing into the farro when it is still warm. Afterward leave it to cool..

4th Step

Pre-heat the grill up to medium/high. Use the salt & the pepper to season the salad

5th Step

Put the chicken in the oven and grill it for between 11 & 15 min; ensuring to turn it once halfway. Leave the chicken to cool for 5 min & then slice it.

6th Step

Mix the fennel & the carrot, as well as the cucumber and onion. Add the parsley, the basil & the mint. Add also 1/3 cup of the salad dressing and mix with the farro.

7th Step

Add the arugula into the mixture of farro. Use you chicken & the olives as topping for your farro mix. Finally, take the remainder of the salad dressing and drizzle it onto the toppings; then proceed to serve.

Nutrition per Single Serving

459 cal/28.2 g protein/31.9 g carbs/5.3 g fiber/4.8 g sugar/24.5 g fat (3.7 g saturated)/62.7 mg cholesterol/4562.4 IU Vitamin A/12.7 mg Vitamin C/38 mcg folate/86.4 mg calcium/2.7 mg iron/44.3 mg magnesium/529.9 mg potassium/512.6 mg sodium/0.1 mg thiamin.

MODIFIED GREEK SALAD

INGREDIENTS: (6 SERVINGS)

Extra virgin olive oil – 2 tbsp

Red wine vinegar – 1 tbsp

Oregano (dried) – 1 tsp

Salt – ¼ tsp

Black pepper – ¼ tsp

Lemon juice – ½ tbsp

Lettuce (chopped) – 2

Cherry tomatoes (in quarters) – 16

Cucumber (sliced) – 1

Kalamata olives (chopped) – 16

Feta cheese – 1 cup (150 g)

METHOD OF PREPARATION: (TOTAL TIME TAKEN: 10 MINUTES)

1st Step

Put the oil, vinegar, oregano in one bowl. Add in salt & pepper plus the lemon juice; and mix properly to make your salad dressing.

2nd Step

Chop up the lettuce, tomatoes, cucumber & the olives and put them into a big bowl. Chop the feta cheese as well and add it in as well.; then mix well to make the salad.

3rd Step

Take the salad and pour it into the bowl with the dressing. Toss the contents to mix everything well and to get the salad well coated with the dressing. Serve your salad.

Nutrition per Single Serving

141 cal/5 g protein/5 g carbs/12 g fat (5 g saturated)/22 mg cholesterol/549 mg sodium/221 mg potassium/1 g fiber/3 g sugar/1224 IU Vitamin A/14 mg Vitamin C/150 mg calcium/1 mg iron.

WATERMELON-RICH FETA CHEESE SALAD

INGREDIENTS: (6 SERVINGS)

Watermelon (diced to 1" thick pieces) – 5 cups

Feta cheese (crumbled) – 2/3 cup

Extra virgin olive oil – 2 tbsp

Extra virgin olive oil – ¼ cup

Capers (rinsed) – ¼ cup

Olives (pitted & halved) – 1/3 cup

Sherry vinegar – 1½ tbsp

Pepper (ground) – sufficient to taste

Basil (fresh & finely sliced) – ½ cup

Mint (fresh & in thin slices) – ½ cup

Almonds (slightly toasted; then sliced) – ¼ cup

Sea salt (flaky) – for garnishing

METHOD OF PREPARATION: (TOTAL TIME TAKEN: 30 MINUTES)

1st Step

Pour 2 tbsp oil into a tiny saucepan and heat it on high. Dry the capers by drying them and then put them into the heated oil

Cook the capers for between 1 & 3 min (the capers should be crisp). Use a slotted spoon to transfer the capers to some paper-lined plate

2nd Step

Pour the remainder of the oil into a big bowl. Add in the olives and vinegar. Add in also the pepper; then whisk the ingredients

Add in the watermelon and the basil plus the mint; then toss to ensure proper coating. Set the salad in a big but shallow serving dish. Sprinkle it with the feta cheese and almonds, as well as the crispy capers. Use the sea salt to garnish the salad.

Nutrition per Single Serving

260 cal/4.4 g protein/12.7 g carbs/1.8 g fiber/8.7 g sugar/22.1 g fat (4.7 g saturated)/14.8 mg cholesterol/1293.8 IU Vitamin A/12.1 mg Vitamin C/22.5 mcg folate/125.2 mg calcium/1.7 mg iron/35.2 mg magnesium/228.5 mg potassium/356 mg sodium.

MEDITERRANEAN SWORDFISH, BEAN & ESCAROLE SALAD

INGREDIENTS: (4 SERVINGS)

Swordfish – 2 pieces of steak (10 oz each)

Escarole (chopped) – 12 cups

White beans (rinsed) – 1 can (15 oz)

Extra virgin olive oil – ¼ cup

Lemon juice – 2 tbsp

Mustard – 1 tsp

Salt – ½ tsp

Pepper (ground) – ½ tsp

Herbes de Provence – 1 tsp

Red onion (finely chopped) – ¼ cup

METHOD OF PREPARATION: (TOTAL TIME TAKEN: 30 MINUTES)

1st Step

Put the rack within the top 3rd of the oven & pre-heat the broiler on high. Spread some foil on some pan that is broiler-safe.

2nd Step

Pour the oil in a big bowl and add in the lemon juice. Add also the mustard plus a ¼ of salt & pepper each. Next, transfer 2 tbsp dressing to some tiny bowl. Put the beans in the big bowl with the dressing; then toss to mix properly.

3rd Step

Slice each of the pieces of steak into halves (meaning there will now be 4 pieces of equal size). Pick the Herbes de Provence and sprinkle it on the swordfish. Sprinkle too the salt and the pepper. Place the fish on the pan already prepared. Broil it from the upper rack for between 8 & 10 min.

4th Step

Toss the escarole plus the onion and the beans. Drizzle the spared dressing (2 tbsp) on the swordfish . Serve.

Nutrition per Single Serving

397 cal/31.5 protein/20.7 g carbs/9.4 g fiber/1.6 g sugar/23 g fat (4 g saturated)/80.7 cholesterol/3386 IU Vitamin A/13.2 mg Vitamin C/291.5 mcg folate/132.8 mg calcium/2.8 mg iron/60.4 mg magnesium/1272.1 mg potassium/66.4 mg sodium/0.2 mg thiamin.

CHAPTER 8:

14 EASY SNACK RECIPES FOR THE MEDITERRANEAN DIET

ROSEMARY-GARLIC PECANS

The savory spiced nuts are the exact ingredient for snacking, if you want to add to a cheese board or serve as a mini appetizer.

INGREDIENTS: (12 SERVINGS)

1 large egg white

2 teaspoons of garlic salt

3 tablespoons of dried rosemary, finely chopped

3 cups of pecans

METHOD OF PREPARATION: (TOTAL TIME TAKEN: 1 HOUR 20 MINUTES)

Step 1

Preheat oven to 250°F.

Step 2

In a bowl, mix the egg white, garlic salt and dried rosemary. Add pecans to it and toss to coat. Spread evenly on a large baking sheet.

Step 3

Bake for 45minutes, but make sure to stir every 15 minutes. Allow it to cool for up to 30 minutes before storing.

Tips

Can be stored in a properly sealed container for about two weeks.

Nutrition per Single Serving

Serving Size: ¼ cup Per Serving: 175 calories; fat 18g; carbohydrates 4g; sodium 332mg; protein 3g; dietary fiber 3g; saturated fat 2g; sugars 1g.

HOMEMADE TRAIL MIX

Try this recipe out with portable mix and any combination of nuts and dried fruits.

INGREDIENTS: (5 SERVINGS)

¼ cup of whole unpeeled shelled almonds

¼ cup of unsalted dry roasted peanuts

¼ cup of dried cranberries

¼ cup of chopped dates

2 ounces of dried apricots, or any other dried fruit

METHOD OF PREPARATION: (TOTAL TIME TAKEN: 5 MINUTES)

Step 1

Mix peanuts, almonds, peanuts, dates, dates and apricots (or any other fruit) in a medium sized bowl.

Tips

Preservation : Make sure to store plastic bags for about 2 weeks at regular room temperature.

Nutrition per Single Serving

Per Serving: 132 calories; carbohydrates 14.8g; protein 3.5g; dietary fiber 2.9g; fat 7.2g; saturated fat 0.8g; sugars 9.8g; vitamin a iu 510.3IU; folate 10.2mcg; calcium 9.9mg; vitamin c 0.3mg; iron 0.4mg; potassium 193.7mg; magnesium 13mg; sodium 0.4mg.

FIG & HONEY YOGURT

In this Mediterranean-inspired snack, honey and dried figs top plain yogurt. If you can find them, substitute fresh figs

INGREDIENTS: (1 SERVINGS)

⅔ cup of low-fat plain yogurt

2 teaspoons of honey

3 dried sliced figs

METHOD OF PREPARATION: (TOTAL TIME TAKEN: 5 MINUTES)

Step 1

Scoop some yogurt in a bowl and top it with honey and figs.

Nutrition per Single Serving

Per Serving: 208 calories; carbohydrates 39.1g; protein 9.4g; dietary fiber 2.5g; fat 2.8g; saturated fat 1.7g; sugars 35.1g; cholesterol 9.8mg; vitamin c 1.7mg; vitamin a iu 85.8IU; folate 20.5mcg; iron 0.7mg; calcium 340.6mg; magnesium 45.2mg; sodium 117.4mg; potassium 560.8mg; added sugar 12g.

SAVORY DATE & PISTACHIO BITES

A taste of sweetness derived from the raisins and dates paired with nuttiness and crunch from the pistachios bring about perfect bites for an an accompaniment on a cheese board or as an on-the-go snack.

INGREDIENTS: (32 SERVINGS)

2 cups of pitted whole dates

1 cup of shelled (unsalted) pistachios

1 cup of golden raisins

1 teaspoon of ground fennel seeds

¼ teaspoon of ground pepper

METHOD OF PREPARATION: (TOTAL TIME TAKEN: 10 MINUTES)

Step 1

Combine pistachios, dates, raisins, pepper and fennel in a food processor. Thenn process till chopped finely. Form into up to 32 balls, using around 1 tablespoon each.

Tips:

To make ahead: Store closed at regular room temperature for about 3 hours.

Nutrition per Single Serving

68 calories; carbohydrates 13.4g; protein 1.1g; dietary fiber 1.4g; fat 1.8g; sugars 10.7g; saturated fat 0.2g; vitamin c 0.4mg; vitamin a iu 37.5IU; folate 3.8mcg; iron 0.3mg; magnesium 12.6mg; calcium 14.7mg; potassium 154.4mg; sodium 0.8mg.

LIME & PARMESAN POPCORN

Ditch the bag filled with microwaved popcorn and satisfy your snack craving by simply making your own lime flavored popcorn. In this healthy popcorn recipe, we use lime zest, parmesan cheese, and a little chili powder, but feel free to use the spices you like the most. For the best flavor, make sure to use olive oil cooking spray to allow the toppings stick to the popcorn.

INGREDIENTS: (1 SERVINGS)

2 cups of plain air-popped popcorn

Olive oil cooking spray

1 tablespoon of Parmesan cheese

1 teaspoon of lime zest

A Pinch of chili powder

A Pinch of salt

METHOD OF PREPARATION: (TOTAL TIME TAKEN: 10 MINUTES)

Step 1

Coat lightly the popcorn with cooking spray; mix with Parmesan, chili powder, lime zest, and salt.

Nutrition per Single Serving

Per Serving: 113 calories; carbohydrates 14.3g; protein 3.5g; dietary fiber 2.6g; fat 5g; sugars 0.2g; saturated fat 1.1g; vitamin a iu 131.1IU; vitamin c 2.6mg; cholesterol 4.3mg; folate 5.6mcg; iron 0.6mg; calcium 47.1mg; magnesium 25.3mg; sodium 243.9mg; potassium 68.2mg.

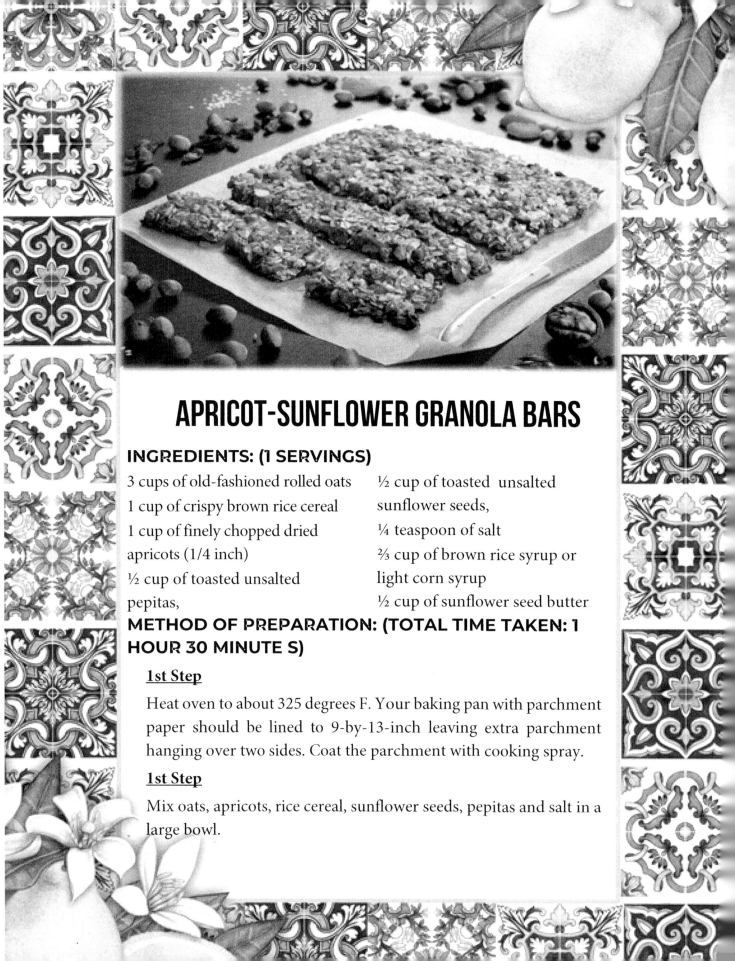

APRICOT-SUNFLOWER GRANOLA BARS

INGREDIENTS: (1 SERVINGS)

3 cups of old-fashioned rolled oats

1 cup of crispy brown rice cereal

1 cup of finely chopped dried apricots (1/4 inch)

½ cup of toasted unsalted pepitas,

½ cup of toasted unsalted sunflower seeds,

¼ teaspoon of salt

⅔ cup of brown rice syrup or light corn syrup

½ cup of sunflower seed butter

METHOD OF PREPARATION: (TOTAL TIME TAKEN: 1 HOUR 30 MINUTE S)

1st Step

Heat oven to about 325 degrees F. Your baking pan with parchment paper should be lined to 9-by-13-inch leaving extra parchment hanging over two sides. Coat the parchment with cooking spray.

1st Step

Mix oats, apricots, rice cereal, sunflower seeds, pepitas and salt in a large bowl.

Step 3

Mix rice syrup (or corn syrup), cinnamon, and sunflower butter in a microwave-safe bowl. Make sure to microwave for 30 seconds (or ensure you heat in a saucepan above medium heat for about 1 minute). Add it to the dry ingredients and stir properly until it's even. Transfer to the prepared pan and press firmly into the pan using the spatula's back.

Step 4

To arrive at chewier bars, make sure to bake until it starts coloring at the edge but still soft in the middle. This will take about 20 to 25 minutes. If you want crunchier bars, bake till it turns golden brown around the edge and still firm in the middle. This will take up to 30 to 35 minutes. (As they cool, they will firm up, although they will first be soft when warm)

Step 5

Let it cool down in the pan for 10 minutes, lift the parchment paper onto a cutting board (it will still be soft). Cut it into 24 bars, then let it cool completely without separating the bars for about 30 minutes more. Once cool, cut into bars.

Tips

Preparation: Individually wrap airtight and store at regular room temperature for about 1 week

Nutrition per Single Serving

Per Serving: 152 calories; carbohydrates 21.5g; protein 3.8g; dietary fiber 2.3g; fat 6.4g; saturated fat 0.8g; sugars 8.8g; vitamin a iu 199IU; vitamin c 0.3mg; calcium 20.4mg; iron 1.1mg; folate 26.2mcg; magnesium 48.8mg; sodium 58.4mg; potassium 230.1mg; added sugar 5g.

CARROT CAKE ENERGY BITES

This amazing snack keep well in the freezer or fridge and are easy to grab on-the-go for a healthy snack.

INGREDIENTS: (22 SERVINGS)

1 cup of pitted dates

½ cup of old-fashioned rolled oats

¼ cup of chopped pecans

¼ cup of chia seeds

2 finely chopped medium carrots

1 teaspoonful of vanilla extract

¾ teaspoonful of ground cinnamon

½ teaspoonful of ground ginger

¼ teaspoonful of ground turmeric

¼ teaspoonful of salt

A Pinch of ground pepper

METHOD OF PREPARATION: (TOTAL TIME TAKEN: 15 MINUTES)

Step 1

Mic dates, pecans, oats, and chia seeds in a food processor; process until well chopped and combined.

Step 2

Add carrots, cinnamon, ginger, vanilla, turmeric, pepper and salt; process till all ingredients are finely chopped and begins to form into paste.

Step 3

Roll the mixture into balls by using a scant 1 Tbsp. each.

Tips

Preservation: Refrigerate in an tightly closed container for about 1 week or freeze for over 3 months.

Nutrition per Single Serving

Per Serving: 48 calories; carbohydrates 8.2g; protein 0.9g; dietary fiber 1.6g; fat 1.7g; saturated fat 0.2g; sugars 5.1g; vitamin a iu 873.8IU; vitamin c 0.3mg; calcium 21.2mg; iron 0.4mg; folate 4.2mcg; potassium 87.6mg; magnesium 14.5mg; sodium 30.4mg.

DATE PISTACHIO GRANOLA BARS

The ingredients in this homemade granola bars are inspired by ingredients that are commonly used in Middle Eastern cooking--dates, hazelnuts, pistachios, cardamoms and tahinis. But you can explore the dried fruit, seeds, nuts, and/or spices to your own preference. Several sticky sweeteners were tested, including maple syrup and honey, but discovered that brown rice syrup could hold the bars together perfectly.

INGREDIENTS: (1 SERVINGS)

3 cups of old-fashioned rolled oats

1 cup of crispy brown rice cereal

1 cup of finely chopped pitted dates, preferably Medjool (1/4 inch)

½ cup toasted and chopped hazelnuts

¼ of teaspoon salt

⅔ cup of brown rice syrup or light corn syrup

½ cup of tahini

1 teaspoon of ground cardamom

METHOD OF PREPARATION: (TOTAL TIME TAKEN: 1 HOUR 30 MINUTES)

Step 1

Heat oven to 325 degrees F. Line a 9-by-13-inch baking pan with parchment paper, leave extra parchment hanging over two sides. Coat the parchment with cooking spray.

Step 2

Mix the oats, rice cereal, dates, hazelnuts, pistachios and salt in a large bowl.

Step 3

Mix the rice syrup (or corn syrup), tahini and cardamom in a microwave-safe bowl. Heat for 30 secs (or heat in a saucepan over medium heat for 1 min). Add it to the dry ingredients and then stir till mixture is even. Transfer it to the prepared pan and press firmly into the pan with the spatula's pan.

Step 4

To make chewier, bake until it starts becoming colored around the edge and yet soft in the middle for about 20 to 25 minutes. If you want it to have crunchier bars, bake until golden brown around the edge and firm in the middle for about 30 to 35 mins. (Both will still be soft when warm and firm up as they cool.)

Step 5

Let it cool in the pan for 10 mins, then using the parchment, lift it out of the pan onto a cutting board (note that it will still be soft). Cut into about 24 bars, then allow it cool completely without separating the bars for up to about 30 minutes more. Once cool, separate them into bars.

Tips

Preservation: Individually wrap in close container and store at regular room temperature for about 1 week.

Nutrition per Single Serving

Per Serving: 155 calories; protein 3.3g; carbohydrates 22.8g; dietary fiber 2.4g; sugars 9.4g; fat 6.4g; saturated fat 0.8g; vitamin a iu 11.3IU; vitamin c 0.5mg , added sugar 5g,; folate 15.7mcg; calcium 25.5mg; iron 0.9mg; magnesium 26mg; potassium 200.6mg; sodium 42mg;

GARLIC HUMMUS

This classic hummus recipe is very easy to make and requires few ingredients in the food processor and whir away! Aquafaba (the liquid in the can of chickpeas) gives it extra smoothness and creaminess .Serve with alongside veggie chips, pita chips or crudités.

INGREDIENTS: (8 SERVINGS)

1 (15 ounce) can of no-salt-added chickpeas

¼ cup of tahini

¼ cup of extra-virgin olive oil

¼ cup of lemon juice

1 clove garlic

1 teaspoonful ofground cumin

½ teaspoonful of chili powder

½ teaspoonful of salt

METHOD OF PREPARATION: (TOTAL TIME TAKEN: 10 MINUTES)

Step 1

Drain chickpeas, reserving a quarter cup of the liquid. Pour the chickpeas and the reserved liquid into a food processor. Add tahini, lemon juice, oil, garlic, chili powder, cumin, and salt. Puree until very smooth for about 2 to 3 minutes.

Nutrition per Single Serving

Per Serving: 155 calories; carbohydrates 9.7g; protein 3.7g; dietary fiber 2.3g; fat 11.9g; saturated fat 1.6g; sugars 0.2g; vitamin a iu 63.4IU; vitamin c 3.4mg; calcium 27.7mg; iron 0.8mg; folate 22mcg; magnesium 15.6mg; sodium 220.6mg; potassium 81.7mg.

EVERYTHING SEASONED ALMONDS

Blend the everything bagel seasoning in a grinder to help it stick to the almonds

INGREDIENTS: (12 SERVINGS)

1 large egg white

3 cups of raw unsalted almonds

3 tablespoonsful of ground everything bagel seasoning

METHOD OF PREPARATION: (TOTAL TIME TAKEN: 1 HOUR 20 MINUTES)

Step 1

Heat oven to 250°F.

Step 2

Whisk egg white and seasoning in a small bowl. Add almonds and flip to coat. Spread evenly on a large rimmed baking sheet.

Step 3

Bake it, while stirring every 15 minutes, until dry, for up to 45 minutes. Let it cool completely before storing, about 30 minutes.

Tips

Preservation: Store in an airtight container for up to 2 weeks.

Nutrition per Single Serving

Per Serving: 223 calories; fat 18g; sodium 245mg; saturated fat 1g, carbohydrates 8g; dietary fiber 4g; protein 8g; sugars 2g;

SENECA WHITE CORN NO BAKE ENERGY BALLS

INGREDIENTS: (36 SERVINGS)

1 ½ of cups quick oats

1 cup of roasted white corn flour (see Tip)

1 teaspoon of ground cinnamon

1 teaspoon of salt

½ cup of natural peanut butter

¼ cup of unsweetened applesauce

2 tablespoons of pure maple syrup

2 – 3 tablespoons of water

2 tablespoons of pure honey

1 teaspoon of vanilla extract

½ cup of unsweetened coconut flakes, plus more for rolling

½ cup of dried fruit, such as raisins and/or currants

½ cup of unsalted roasted mixed chopped nuts, like pecans, almonds, walnuts and/or hazelnuts

METHOD OF PREPARATION: (TOTAL TIME TAKEN: 15 MINUTES)

Step 1

Line a baking pan with parchment paper.

Step 2

Mix oats, corn flour, cinnamon and salt in a bowl. Pour in peanut butter, maple syrup, apple sauce, 2 tablespoons water, vanilla and honey. Gently stir in coconut flakes, dried fruit and nuts.

Step 3

Use clean hands to roll the mixture into 1-inch balls, using about 1 heaping tablespoon to make each. (If the mixture is too dry to roll, stir in 1 tablespoon water.) Roll in coconut as desired

Tip

You can purchase roasted white corn flour from Gakwi:yo:h Farms online at shop.senecamuseum.org.

Nutrition per Single Serving

Per Serving: 77 calories; protein 2g; carbohydrates 9g; dietary fiber 1g; selenium 1mcg,sugars 3g; added sugar 2g; fat 4g; saturated fat 1g; mono fat 2g; poly fat 1g; vitamin a iu 1IU; folate 12mg; sodium 77mg; calcium 10mg; iron 1mg; magnesium 8mg; phosphorus 17mg; potassium 32mg; niacin equivalents 4mg.

KALE CHIPS

Don't like kale? These crispy baked kale chips will change your mindset For the best result, don't put too much in the pans.

INGREDIENTS: (4 SERVINGS)

1 large bunch of kale, tough stems removed, leaves torn into pieces (about 16 cups;)

1 tablespoon of extra-virgin olive oil

¼ teaspoon of salt

METHOD OF PREPARATION: (TOTAL TIME TAKEN: 25 MINUTES)

Step 1

Place racks in upper third as well as center of oven; preheat oven to 400 degrees F.

Step 2

If kale is wet, pat dry using a clean kitchen towel; tehn transfer to a large bowl. Make sure to drizzle the kale with oil and also sprinkle with salt. Using hands, massage the oil and salt ino the kale leaves to coat evenly. Fill 2 large rimmed baking sheets with one layer of kale while making sure that the leaves do not overlap. (If the kale won't all fit, do the chips in batches.)

Step 3

Bake until crisp, switch the pans back to front and top to bottom halfway through for a total of 8 to 12 minutes . (Start checking after 8 minutes to prevent burning, if baking a batch on just one sheet)

Nutrition per Single Serving

Per Serving: 110 calories; carbohydrates 15.8g; protein 5.3g; iron 2.5mg; magnesium 50.7mg; sodium 210.1mg; thiamin 0.2mg; potassium 641.6mg; dietary fiber 5.6g; fat 4.6g; saturated fat 0.6g; sugars 3.5g; vitamin a iu 38329.5IU; vitamin c 115.4mg; calcium 202.7mg folate 36.6mcg.

CURRIED CASHEW

This snack is very addictive as its exhausted in a twinkling of an eye. Don't use salt , if you will make use of salted cashews.

INGREDIENTS: (48 SERVINGS)

6 tablespoons of lemon juice

6 tablespoons of curry powder

4 teaspoons of kosher salt

6 cups og unsalted cashews

METHOD OF PREPARATION: (TOTAL TIME TAKEN: 50 MINUTES)

Step 1

Arrange racks in the upper and lower thirds of your oven; preheat the oven to 250 degrees F.

Step 2

Mix lemon juice, curry powder and salt in a large bowl. Add cashews; flip to coat. Divide between 2 large rimmed baking sheets; spread evenly.

Step 3

Bake, stirring every 15 mins, until dry for , about 45 mins. Let cool completely. Store in airtight container.

Tips

Preservation: Store in an airtight container for up to 3 weeks.

Nutrition per Single Serving

Per Serving: 101 calories; protein 2.7g; iron 1.2mg; magnesium 46.5mg; potassium 107.5mg; sodium 96.5mg.carbohydrates 6.2g; dietary fiber 0.9g; sugars 0.9g; fat 8.1g; saturated fat 1.6g; vitamin a iu 0.3IU; vitamin c 0.7mg; folate 12.6mcg; calcium 11.8mg

TUNA SALAD SPREAD

This is a healthy go to spread in which Greek yoghurt is used in place of mayonnaise. It can be served with butter lettuce leaves, whole grains and avocado.

INGREDIENTS: (4 SERVINGS)

1 mashed avocado

2 tablespoons of low-fat plain Greek yogurt

1 tablespoon of lemon juice

1 tablespoon of chopped fresh parsley

¼ teaspoon of garlic powder

¼ teaspoon of paprika

¼ teaspoon of salt

¼ teaspoonful of ground pepper

1 (5 ounce) can albacore tuna in water, drained

¼ cup of diced onion or celery

METHOD OF PREPARATION: (TOTAL TIME TAKEN: 5 MINUTES)

Step 1

Mix avocado and yogurt in a small bowl and stir well. Add lemon juice, parsley, garlic powder, paprika, salt and pepper and stir well. Add tuna and onion (or celery) and mix gently until well combined.

Nutrition per Single Serving

Per Serving: sodium174.6mg, potassium 281.7mg, magnesium 17.5mg, iron 0.4mg, calcium19.1mg, folate 45.8mcg, vitamin C 8.6mg, vitamin a in 225.4IU, cholesterol 16.5mg, saturated fat 1.2g, fat 8.2g, sugars1.1g, dietary fibre3.7g, carbohydrates 6.1g, protein 10.1g, 130 calories

CHAPTER 9

FREQUENTLY ASKED QUESTIONS

Question: Is it possible to lose weight through the Mediterranean diet?

Answer: Yes, it is!

When people live on a Mediterranean diet, it is possible for them to lose weight that is either equivalent to the amount they would lose on a low-carb or low-fat diet.

Research has linked the Mediterranean diet to reduced body fat; meaning the diet is great for minimizing weight increase. You can live on the Mediterranean diet for your entire lifetime and reap the great benefits of keeping chronic ailments and other health conditions at bay.

Nevertheless, you need to keep certain principles in mind when it comes to weight maintenance. The major ones include the importance of consuming your dinner early in the day as opposed to late evening; ensuring the greatest proportion of your meals comprises vegetables; avoiding consumption of processed food items, especially when they are starchy; and consuming lots of water and herbal drinks.

Question: What is the easiest way to reduce consumption of meat?

Answer: For those who love to eat meat on a daily basis, there is no need for worry. You can still eat meat but in smaller quantities that are prepared differently.

Question: Is it alright for a vegan to rely on the Mediterranean diet?

Answer: It is! What many people do not know is that the Mediterranean diet as originally used by the Greeks was a vegan model for a good part of the year, in adherence to religion. The role of meat in the Mediterranean diet is actually secondary, and for that reason the cuisines are dominated by vegan choices. These include the sumptuous vegetable meals, different bean-based recipes, vegetable-dominated patties and dips.

If you are a vegan, you can also supplement your diet with nuts, such as walnuts, and also grains and seeds.

Question: Does the Mediterranean diet offer options that are free from gluten?

Answer: Sure, it does. Most of the Mediterranean dishes are dominated by vegetables, and so there is a wide variety of them whose ingredients have no gluten.

Apart from the pasta dishes and a few spicy pies, most of the dishes under the Mediterranean diet happen to be gluten-free.

Moreover, studies have indicated that people who have celiac disease and choose to avoid gluten are able to meet their nutritional needs for the greatest part if they rely on the Mediterranean diet; yet they manage to control their weight.

Question: Is it alright to live on a Mediterranean diet when I'm diabetic?

Answer: Yes, it is. Although the Mediterranean diet is best known for heart health, it is great too for fighting diabetes.

There has been research linking the Mediterranean diet to weight management, regulation of blood glucose, and delayed need for diabetics to go on medication. The effectiveness of this diet has actually been found to be greater than many other diets hailed for health enhancement.

It should be noted that the Mediterranean diet is low on carbohydrates, contains healthy fats, and incorporates whole grains. Great still is the fact that the diet is dominated by vegetables. This combination serves to stabilize the level of sugar in the blood.

The Mediterranean diet is also heavy on antioxidants; hence it plays a major role in preventing diabetes among other ailments.

Question: Is alcohol part of the Mediterranean diet?

Answer: Not necessarily. Anyone who does not partake of alcohol need not begin when they go on the Mediterranean diet.

For those who do, they need to restrict themselves to red wine and take it in moderation to accompany meals. In short, not taking wine or any other kind of alcohol does not diminish the benefits of the Mediterranean diet.

Question: Is the Mediterranean diet good for the entire family?

Answer: Yes, it is. Research has shown that kids fed on the Mediterranean diet normally maintain normal weight. That is the same case for women who are pregnant.

It is important to note that the vegetable incorporated in the diet normally have great flavor, and everyone, including kids, find then palatable.

CONCLUSION

Doctors and nutritionists all over the globe are in agreement that any diet with saturated fats is not good for health. In fact, a diet with a high level of saturated fat can lead to heart ailments, cancer, and other health issues.

The reason the Mediterranean diet is so popular is its low level of saturated fats. On average, the calories people who adhere to the Mediterranean diet derive from their meals comprise below 8% from risky saturated fats.

This percentage is well below the dangerous saturated fat level that provides calories to the average person consuming an ordinary diet.

As you seek to enjoy great health from the Mediterranean diet, keep in mind the most important ingredients to incorporate in your meals.

Must-have Ingredients for Your Mediterranean Recipes

Vegetables

Note that you can incorporate almost any type of vegetable into your Mediterranean diet. There are different ways of preparing these vegetables. While some are best consumed raw, others may be steamed or roasted using olive oil.

Vegetables are also great when accompanied with onions, tomatoes, garlic and herbs. The commonest vegetables for the Mediterranean diet include cabbage, cucumber, broccoli and carrots; as well as beet, cauliflower, okra and leeks.

Other popular vegetables in the Mediterranean diet include celery and eggplant, green beans, mushroom and peas, potatoes, peppers and zucchini.

Green Vegetables

There is an important place for greens in the Mediterranean diet, especially considering how rich they are in anti-oxidants. For that reason, you are better off stocking your pantry with greens such as arugula and chicory, dandelions, kale and lettuce, and even spinach.

Fruits

It is recommended that you incorporate seasonal fruits into your diet, because they give you the best flavor. Buying fresh fruits, such as apples, lemons and apricots, or even avocado, cherries and cantaloupe is a good option.

Other great fruits to buy when in season include figs, tangerines and mandarins, grapefruit and grapes, oranges, raisins and peaches, and even pears, dates, apricots and watermelon.

Nuts & Oil

It is crucial that you only buy extra virgin olive oil of great quality. Also, the nut used in the Mediterranean diet ought to be unsalted.

It is recommended that in addition to the extra virgin olive oil, you also stock your pantry with pine nuts and pistachios, walnuts and tahini, as well as sesame seeds.

It is also advised that you avoid any vegetable or seed oil, and that includes canola, and the varieties from corn and soybeans.

Beans

It is preferable to use dry beans in the Mediterranean diet, although it is alright to use the canned type.

The variety of beans to avoid is the baked kind and any of those types with added fat, and any beans with any other unwanted additions.

You can also buy black-eyed peas that are uncooked, butter beans, white beans and pinto beans, or even chickpeas and lentils.

Grains & Bread

You are advised to find whole grain bread, or even pita bread, which have no additives or preservatives, and those that have no unhealthy fats.

Whole grain pasta is acceptable; but you should expect it to have a different texture. The type of rice recommended is the medium-grain, the one whose texture is creamy. It is advisable to avoid the short-grain type of rice, as it is usually very sticky. Long grain rice has the disadvantage of usually being too dry.

Brown rice is appropriate in the Mediterranean diet, although you should anticipate its cooking time to be longer. At the same time, this kind of rice may not produce your favorable texture.

You may also incorporate grains like barley, couscous and bulgur wheat in your Mediterranean dishes.

Dairy Products

Yogurt, especially Greek yogurt in its plain state, is recommended, whether it is derived from cow or goat milk; also whether it is high in fat or not.

The most important thing in this case is to select milk with no fillers or gelatin, or even stabilizers. Just as important is selecting milk with no flavoring, sweetener or protein.

When choosing cheese to incorporate in the Mediterranean diet, it is a good idea to identify a type that is rich in fat, such as feta or Parmesan cheese, mizithra or ricotta, or even mozzarella. If you choose to use feta cheese, it is recommended you find the one derived from sheep milk; not cow milk.

Meat & Poultry

You need to select meat or poultry meat from animals fed on grass; whether it is veal, beef, pork or lamb.

As for poultry, you can choose whole chicken or just pieces of chicken. It is recommended that you avoid use of processed meat; and even deli meat like bacon, sausages, salami and bologna.

Seafood; including Fish

You can make use of fish that is fresh or even frozen. The most popularly used fish in the Mediterranean diet include sardines and salmon, trout, mackerel and anchovies, and even herring. The fatty fish is the most preferred.

Other fish often incorporated into the Mediterranean recipes include crayfish and crab, octopus and lobster, and even shrimp.

Things you Need in Your Pantry

Make sure you have olives processed the Greek way, because these are very high in anti-oxidants. Honey is another item you need in your pantry when you are living on a Mediterranean diet. You need to make it your basic sweetener as opposed to cane sugar or such other sugars.

Balsamic vinegar and tomatoes that have been crushed and canned, capers and kalamata olives, tomatoes that have been sundried and red wine vinegar are other useful items to have.

You also need to have in stock natural spices and herbs such as basil, parsley and black pepper, dill and cumin, ground cinnamon, oregano and mint as well as sea salt & kosher salt.

All in all, you are on the path to keeping ailments at a minimum if you live on a Mediterranean diet; a diet whose recipes are easy and convenient to prepare, and one that is generally affordable.

Printed in Great Britain
by Amazon

18868626R00086